Orientation

Reading Earth's Mysteries Through Human Perception

Gary Liu

2026

Published by Gary\Liu [Melbourne, Australia]

First published 2026

ISBN: 978-1-7646347-1-7 (paperback version)

Disclaimer: This book is intended for informational purposes only.

Contents

Introduction

This book is not asking you to believe anything. It is asking you to notice how things are being seen.

Most books about unexplained phenomena ask: *What is this?*

This book asks a different question first: *From what kind of perception is this being seen?*

That shift changes everything. What follows is not a catalogue of beliefs, nor an attempt to explain the world's mysteries. It is an exploration of the structures that underlie them — and a demonstration that when you change the lens, the same phenomena start to look very different.

How This Perception Developed

Before describing the lens, it is worth saying something about where it came from — because readers will reasonably ask.

The structural method used in this book was not learned as a technique. It was not accessed through belief, spiritual practice, or visualisation. It emerged gradually as a byproduct of sustained psychological work.

Extended Jungian shadow work — years of remaining present with conflicting interpretations, emotional charge, and unresolved meaning without prematurely collapsing them into story — trained a particular kind of internal stability. Over time, this created an environment where narratives could be held without being inhabited. The ability to sit with something without immediately reaching for what it means.

Once that narrative pressure reduced sufficiently, something else began to register. Not images. Not messages. Simple structural constraints — relational configurations that limited what could reasonably arise from a given situation. The shapes described throughout this book are what that perceiving produces.

They are not symbolic. They are not personal. They function as orientation markers that appear when interpretation is suspended long enough for underlying structure to become evident.

This way of perceiving is not presented as special or rare. It is a consequence of learning how not to interfere with meaning while it is forming. Whether others can develop similar perception is an open question this book does not attempt to answer. What it does offer is the consistent application of that perception across a wide range of phenomena — so that the mappings can be evaluated on their own terms.

The Lens This Book Uses

The phenomena in this book are read through a simple structural framework. Information is described in terms of shapes and their position relative to a central human axis — left, centre, and right.

These three zones each carry a distinct quality:
• Left is the relational and ecological domain. It is where information exists between things rather than inside isolated objects. Distributed, receptive, non-linear. This is the domain of felt connection, environmental sensing, and knowledge that

doesn't arrive through reasoning. For example, walking into a room with people and feeling the vibe of the room.

- Centre is the human domain. It is not a zone but a line — the place where left and right are held together, mediated, and lived. It is load-bearing. When it is functioning well, a person can carry both relational depth and structured thought without either collapsing.

- Right is the domain of abstraction, systems, and structured output. Organisation, hierarchy, effort, and formal knowledge originate here. This is where analysis happens, where things get built, and where conclusions are drawn.

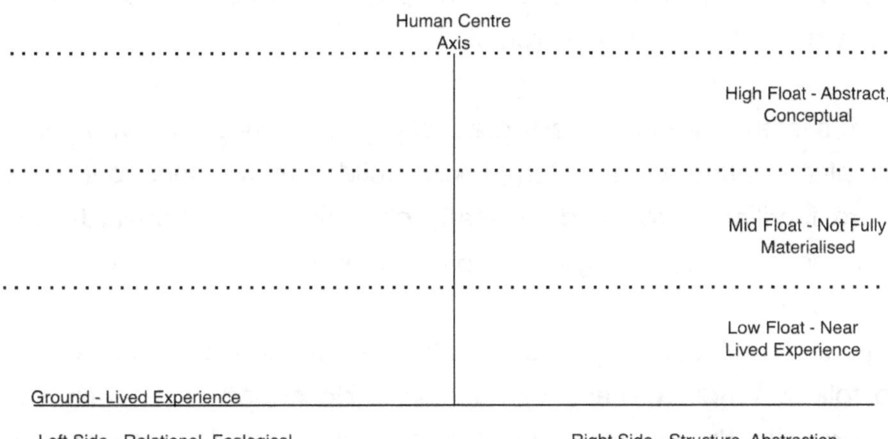

Most people reading this book will be more familiar with the right side than the left. Modern culture runs predominantly through right-side channels — science, institutions, interpretation, narrative. The left side is not absent from modern life, but it is largely unrecognised and under-used.

This matters because many of the phenomena in this book — ancient sites, mythic figures, strange places, reported encounters

— make little sense through a right-side lens alone. They were produced by, or belong to, a different mode of perception. Reading them through structure rather than story is what allows them to become coherent.

How the Book Is Structured

Each chapter applies this lens to a specific phenomenon — an ancient site, a mythic figure, a reported encounter, a place of high strangeness, a mysterious artefact.

The approach is consistent throughout: a structural pattern is presented first, then mapped to the phenomenon, then followed to see what naturally follows from it.

The system is introduced gradually. Early chapters work with simpler configurations. Complexity builds as the lens becomes more familiar. If you find the early chapters straightforward, stay with them — they are laying the ground for what comes later.

The book includes diagrams to make the spatial descriptions easier to follow. When a shape or position is described in the text, the diagram is there to anchor it concretely. You do not need to memorise the system. It becomes recognisable through use.

If you read ahead looking for conclusions, the book may feel strange or incomplete. If you allow each configuration to register before reaching for interpretation, the mapping often becomes self-evident — even when it leads somewhere unexpected.

What This Book Is Not

It is not a spiritual teaching. It is not a theory requiring acceptance. It does not ask you to adopt a belief system or abandon the one you have.

It is closer to a field report from a cartographer who has been mapping territory that is usually passed over — and who is leaving markers so that others can find their way through the same ground.

What This Book Is Saying

At its simplest:
Here is a way of relating to reality that has been largely under-inhabited — and here is what becomes visible when you enter it.

By the end, the most important thing the book may offer is not an answer to the mysteries it examines, but a different way of noticing — one that makes the real questions clearer than they were before.

This book was written through direct observation, reflection, and synthesis. Language tools were occasionally used for clarity and editing. The framework, interpretations, and structure are the author's.

Ancient Sites

Göbekli Tepe

Gobekli Tepe is an ancient site that is baffling archaeologists around the world. It is located in southeastern Turkey, excavated from inside a low hill. The site's fully constructed foundation structure was dated to be built around 9600 BC (12,000 years ago). There is evidence that subsequent generations of humans have layered their own construction on the site to suit the needs of their time.

The earliest layers included massive T-shaped limestone pillars, with some stones weighing 20 tonnes. And arranged in circular enclosures. Intricate carved animal reliefs are part of the site. What challenges prevailing archaeological models is that humans in 9600 BC are generally thought to be nomadic hunter gatherers, with limited social hierarchy. And structures associated with these groups are temporary.

Meaning the earliest layers were built prior to settled civilisation (by conventional definition) - no agriculture, pottery, and metal tools. And what's more, later layers showed smaller pillars, cruder workmanship, and less complexity, suggesting a decline in capacity rather than linear technological progress. Then to top off the icing on the baffling cake, the entire site was buried after centuries of use!

Key questions that are unresolved:
• How were 20 tonne stones quarried and moved?

- How was the scale of coordination achieved to build the site?
- Why is there evidence of geometric planning at such an early age of humanity?
- Why did technical sophistication decline over time?
- Why was the entire site intentionally buried?

— —

Pattern Reading

To get insight into these questions, Gobekli Tepe is read as a relational pattern. The question is: In relation to human orientation, which is represented by a central axis, what is the distribution of effort and knowledge?

These shapes appear simultaneously, indicating coexistence rather than succession. Sensed relational pattern:

- Off-centre right: Straight line which slopes ~40° to the right
- Far left: Small, faded, floating circle

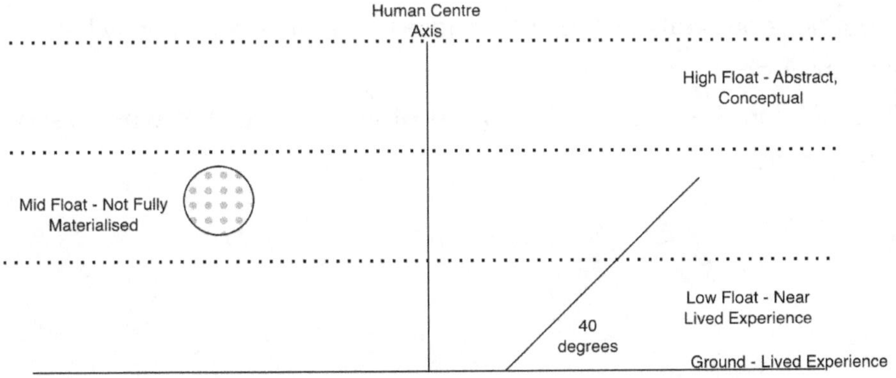

— —

Pattern Interpretation

Off-centre right: Straight line which slopes ~40° to the right

A sloping straight line indicates sustained effort over a long period of time. It represents pragmatic, functional work. And organised communal effort sustained through repetition rather than innovation.

This suggests purposeful construction. Neither defensive in nature nor residential. Likely ritual use, communal, or orientation use.

Far left: Small, faded, floating circle

A circle indicates integrated knowing. It being on the left side indicates it is coherent but non-structural knowledge.
Small means limited access, possibly to a shrinking cohort of humans.
Faded means the knowledge was already in decline.
Floating represents not fully embodied, or stabilised, in daily life. (ie. not grounded)
The builders had access to a form of knowledge that was already weakening.

— —

Mapping Pattern to Site Features

The left side knowledge maps cleanly to the otherwise unexplained capacity to coordinate, move, and place massive stones without evidence of mechanical infrastructure. And to the layout of the site in line with geometric planning.

The fading aspect reflects the decline of the technical sophistication over time. There was gradual loss of this knowledge. Reliance increasingly shifted to effort over time.

Once the knowledge was fully faded, the site became "irrelevant", or impractical to operate and use. Burying it shows that the humans at the time thought it was worth preserving, rather than destroying it. Preserving it as form, after function was lost.

Gobekli Tepe likely does not represent the dawn of civilisation. Instead it suggests a late stage expression of an earlier capacity that subsequently faded. Sustained effort was compensating for fading knowledge. It represents a society already in transition, operating with diminishing access to a form of knowledge or knowing. Not primitive beginnings, but possibly late attempt to preserve something older.

Similar patterns appears across other ancient sites around the world. This points to a broader transition in human capability.

Easter Island Statues

Giant stone human statues ("Moai statues") made from volcanic rock line a geographically isolated island. The island is Easter

Island, 3,500km from South America, and 2,000km from the nearest inhabited island.

There are nearly 1,000 Moai statues on the island, each 4-10 metres in height, with some larger. And can weigh up to 80 tonnes. They were dated to being carved between 1200-1600AD.

Archaeologists' research revealed the Moai were made from volcanic rock from the Rano Raraku quarry, and transported all around the island to rest on stone platforms (called the "Ahu"). The Moai are often found along the coast, facing inland. Their making was eventually abandoned and many statues were toppled.

Key questions that are unresolved:

- With a small, isolated population, and no metal tools, draft animals or wheeled vehicles, how did they carve and transport so many statues around the island? With much of the terrain uneven volcanic rock.
- Why did the population invest sustained, multi-generational effort in creating the Moai? There are no obvious defensive, economic or utilitarian function associated with the Moai.
- Why were the Moai eventually abandoned and toppled?

— —

Pattern Reading 1 — Easter Island Statues

Shapes Sensed
- Off-centre right: straight uphill slope (~30°)
- Left side, low height: mid-sized floating horizontal solid rectangle

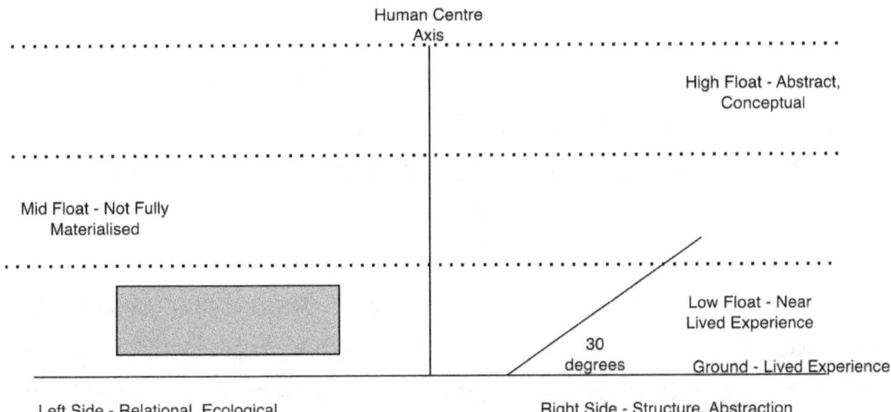

Pattern Interpretation

Off-centre right: straight uphill slope (~30°)

On the right side, a straight and uphill slope reflects sustained, linear and cumulative effort. Which requires coordinated, and often repetitive effort needing endurance. Indicates labour driven work.

Left side, low height: mid-sized floating horizontal solid rectangle

Represents a stabilising structure rather than something in motion. A rectangle is associated with balance, grounding and alignment. Low height indicates diminished potency.
Floating means no longer fully embedded in lived daily coherence.

Combined, it means it was a cultural output, driven primarily by effort and coordination. It was reliant on a residual stabilising framework that had diminished potency and was already weakening.

Mapping Pattern to the Site

Recent archaeological theory is that the Moai were "walked" to their locations via ropes and shifting them side to side. This large scale coordination and sustained communal labour involved is supported by the uphill slope shape.

The left side rectangle maps to the Moai being placed on Ahu, stabilising platforms. And that the statues represent faces of ancestors, looking inland, as relational anchors over the inhabitants of the island.

Floating quality suggests the practice of creating the Moai continued beyond the conditions that made them naturally optimised. Meaning it was likely ritualised repetition.

The abandonment and toppling of the Moai signals the failure point of the left side stabilising rectangle. Not random destruction. It was the collapse of stabilising field, rather than collapse of society per se.

— —

Pattern Reading 2 — What was the Purpose of the Moai?

A second reading was performed to get insight into the purpose of the Moai.

Shape Sensed
Off-centre left: Grounded and mostly vertical curve. Curves toward centre axis but does not touch it.

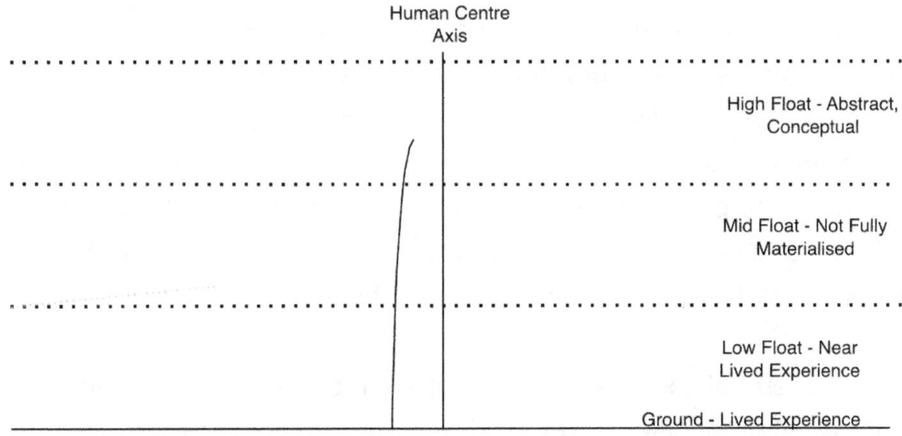

Pattern Interpretation

The left side represents shared relational knowing, rather than effort or measured output. In this scenario, the relational knowing would be landed based, and ancestors oriented.

Grounded means still embodied, not abstract.

Curve implies adaptive, responsive, and accomodating. Curving towards the centre but not touching means attempting to remain connected to and support human coherence, but the connection is weakening and not fully accessible.

Mapping Pattern to the Site

The Moai are not exerting power or authority. They are not for defensive purposes, nor for signalling outward. They were not monuments of excess. They face inland to watch over the people. Symbolically - ancestors watching over their descendants.

They are external, symbolic, orientation anchors. Of relational coherence. With the land and ancestors. References for a relationship humans were beginning to lose internally. The patterns suggest that the Moai were constructed during a period when relational orientation was declining, and the community was using externalised, physical forms to stabilise what they could no longer fully sustain internally. They are evidence of a culture attempting to stabilise relational coherence before that capacity was lost.

This pattern of externalised relational stabilisation shows up at a number of other sites like Gobekli Tepe and Avebury Stones.

The Lost Labyrinth of Hawara

The Labyrinth of Hawara dates back to 1800BC, located near the pyramid of Amenemhat III, south of Cairo. Once a vast structure measuring roughly 300 by 250 metres across two levels, it is now considered "lost" due to dismantling during the Roman and Ptolemaic periods and chronic flooding from rising groundwater. This makes archeological excavation extremely difficult.

In history, there has been eyewitness accounts - from Herodotus, Strabo, Diodorus, reporting that there were two levels. One upper, one subterranean with 1500 rooms in each. The whole structure was covered by monolithic slabs of stone. The interior was confusing and difficult to navigate without guidance.

Key questions that are unresolved:
• Why the huge investment of effort into something that was not monumental, defensive, efficient in layout? The defining feature appears to be disorientation.

- Why is there no central axis, no commanding viewpoint?

— —

Pattern Reading

Shapes sensed
Off-centre left: A covered large labyrinth-like form. Grounded and faded.

— —

Pattern Interpretation

Left-side emphasis indicates relational knowing: Participation over instruction. Experience over explanation. As opposed to the right side which emphasises effort over time and centralised authority.

With the large labyrinth-like form being covered, it has no bird's eye view available. No position from which the whole can be understood. This means that meaning only arises through traversing it. Not by observing.

The labyrinth form implies multiplicity over hierarchy. Many pathways with no dominant route. A distributed structure. Designed to hold people within relations, not move them efficiently through.

Grounded means embedded in land and daily life of the culture in which it was built. The knowledge was lived. Not conceptualised.

Faded means decline, but not yet absent. The labyrinth preserves a capacity already weakening. Hawara is not an expression of peak architectural ability. It is a compensatory structure.

Hawara functions as a memory substrate. It does not organise people. It organises perception.

— —

Mapping Pattern to the Site

Navigation through a labyrinth is inherently disorienting, as historic eyewitness accounts of the Hawara Labyrinth repeatedly describe. Traversal requires memory, continuous choice, and relational awareness. Orientation cannot be outsourced to a map or a single reference point. Meaning emerges only through embodied movement.

The architecture does not clarify. It demands participation. This suggests the labyrinth was not designed to confuse for its own sake, but to reinforce an internal human capacity that was becoming unreliable. Architecture was used to externalise orientation — not to teach it, but to require it.

What was being lost was not a belief system, nor a forgotten technology, but a way human orientation itself functioned.

To traverse the Hawara Labyrinth, a person had to remain aware of multiple pathways without privileging a dominant route. Progress depended on sensing relationships between spaces, remembering prior movement, and staying coherent without a fixed centre of reference.

This mode of navigation reflects what this book calls "distributed orientation".

On a larger scale, this implies that orientation was not held solely within individuals. It was lived rather than thought. Meaning was distributed across land, movement, structure, and shared participation. The labyrinth did not provide direction — it revealed whether orientation was still intact.

As distributed orientation weakened in humans, the labyrinth stopped training perception, and instead began producing confusion. The labyrinth didn't fail. Humans changed. With the result being dismantling and abandonment.

Gobekli Tepe shows distributed orientation weakening but still accessible. Easter Island Statues reveals compensation through effort as orientation declined. And Hawara represents an attempt to preserve orientation by embedding it directly into architecture.

(Author's clarification: Distributed orientation is a subjective experience of ancient peoples. As such, its meaning could not be fully recovered. The repeating spatial and architectural signatures of ancient sites looked at in this book only allows functional inference. An analogy is embodied learning of martial arts. Knowledge is transmitted through movement and hands on correction by a master, not explanation alone.)

Derinkuyu

In 1963, a local man in Turkey was renovating his home. He knocked down a wall in his basement, and to his surprise, found himself in a forgotten room that led to a tunnel. The tunnel led to one of the most impressive engineering marvels of the ancient world. He stumbled upon Derinkuyu.

Derinkuyu is a multi-level ancient subterranean city located in Cappadocia, Turkey. It extends 80 metres underground and houses multiple rooms, tunnels, ventilation shafts that support the city, and heavy rolling stone doors. It appeared to be built for survival and concealment, with archaeologists identifying food storage areas, communal areas and well. It can house tens of thousands of people.

Dating estimates vary widely, ranging from the first millennium BC to much earlier periods. What matters for this analysis is not the absolute date, but the conditions the structure responds to, being pressure, concealment, and long-term habitation.

Key questions that are unresolved:

- How was such a structure possible?
- Why build underground when surface settlements were viable and probably the norm?
- What function did complexity and concealment serve?

— —

Pattern Reading

The site is read relationally, looking at the distribution of effort, knowledge, and orientation. Shapes reflect capacities present, whether they were preserved or degrading.

Shapes sensed:
- Bottom centre - Slightly right tilted rising line
- Far left - Tall solid, and grounded, unfaded pillar
- Off-centre left - Small grounded half faded circle
- Mid-left - Large floating faded pyramid

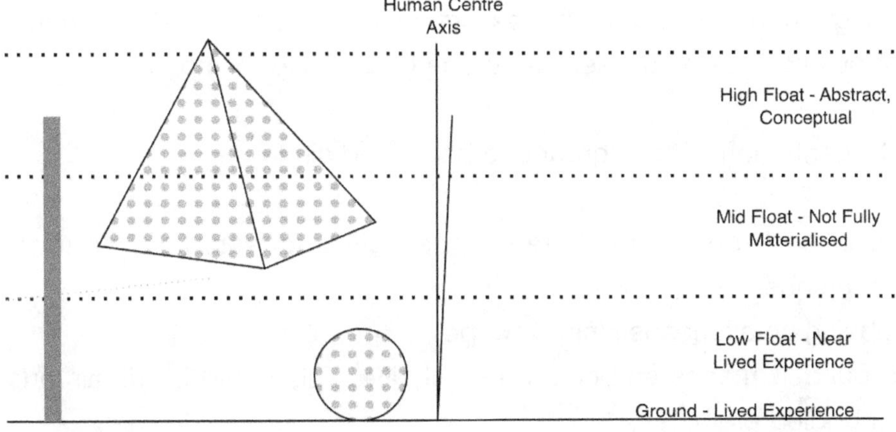

— —

Pattern Interpretation

Bottom centre - Slightly right tilted rising line

Right tilt indicates pragmatic, effort based organisation. Right side means this takes place under structure and driven by logistics.
As it touches the centre human centric axis, it suggests survival driven necessity. Survival here does not mean temporary escape. It implies continuity. Keeping something alive long enough to be transmitted.

Far left - Tall solid, and grounded, unfaded pillar

Left side means relational, distributed orientation.
Vertical means it relates to lineage, continuity, and transmission.
Solid, grounded and unfaded indicates it was a capacity that was still alive at the time of construction and / or use.
This is deliberate preservation. Not decay. Derinkuyu protected a living left-side capacity. It was likely limited to a cohort, not entire population. It was a selective refuge for a way of being human.

Off-centre left - Small grounded half faded circle

Localised and diminished / partially accessible relational coherence.
It being small means limited scope.
Grounded means embedded in daily life. This could be rituals and embodied practices.

Mid-left - Large floating faded pyramid

A dominant influence on the left side, with the pyramid representing hierarchy, authority, and formal systems. Faded implies firmly dominant, and declining influence. Floating means the pyramid was not grounded, disconnected from the relational field.

The pyramid represents an external surface civilisation - hierarchical, abstracted, and authority driven - whose expansion made distributed orientation untenable in open environments. A civilisation whose influence is not embedded in Derinkuyu itself.

The overall pattern is of preservation under pressure.

What Derinkuyu is not: A short term bunker, religious sanctuary, seat of power, or a retreat for elites.

— —

Mapping Pattern to the Site

Derinkuyu appears to have been built primarily using labour and effort, with some left side environmental relational knowledge, explaining why such a structure can survive for so long in a good shape.

The city resembles a labyrinth in layout, with no major centres of power. This kind of architecture appears similar to the Lost Labyrinth of Hawara in that architecture was used as externalised orientation. It requires participation and relational awareness.

Derinkuyu is not a marvel of engineering for its own sake. It is a survival vessel for a way of orienting that could no longer exist on the surface. It shelters a way of being human that could no longer survive openly, in an above ground society that leans on hierarchy, authority, and formal systems.

Where earlier sites in this book attempted to stabilise or preserve orientation through monuments and architecture, Derinkuyu represents the moment when orientation had to be hidden in order to persist at all.

The Pyramids and the Sphinx

There are not many ancient structures that are as well known as the pyramids and the Great Sphinx, located in the desert at the Giza Plateau in Egypt. Mainstream archaeology dates the site to approximately 4,500 years ago, though some geological and astronomical analyses suggest the complex may preserve alignments from much earlier periods.

The largest of the three pyramids, Khufu (the other two being Khafre and Menkaure) is 150 metres tall, made from over two million blocks of 2-3 tonnes each. The pyramids were built with extreme geometric precision, still considered advanced by modern standards.

Adjacent to the pyramids is the Great Sphinx, carved from the area's bedrock. It is 73 metres long, with a lion body and human head.

— —

Pattern Reading 1 — The Pyramids

The pyramid complex (excluding the Sphinx, which will have its own reading) is read as a single relational system.

Shapes Sensed

- Three grounded vortices — left, centre, right
- On the centre axis: A solid, medium sized pyramid

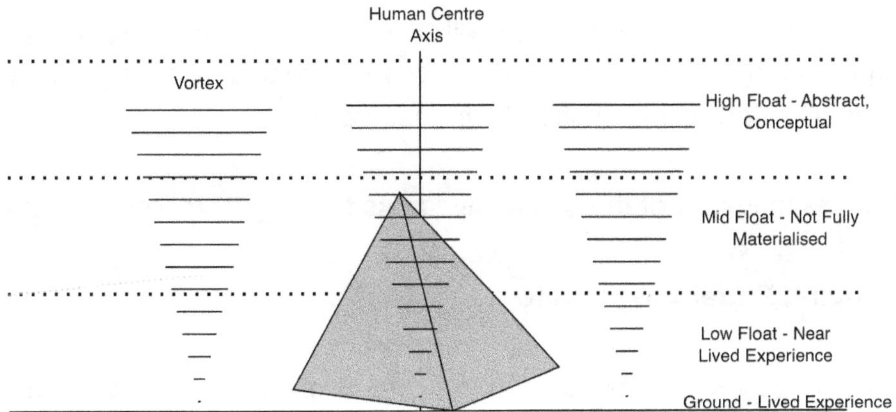

Pattern Interpretation

Three grounded vortices

A vortex demonstrates flow and transformation.
Grounded means anchored and expressed in reality.
Left vortex maintains harmony of the relational field, between land and people.

Centre vortex stabilises human coherence and mediation between left and right.
Right vortex formalises knowledge and the system into a durable structure (ie. the pyramids).
All three vortices and sides are balanced.

On the centre axis: A solid, medium sized pyramid

Symbolises authority, permanence, and formalised pattern
Anchors the relational balance between left, centre and right. The centre in this framework is not a domain, but a line of human coherence. Structures appearing on it are stabilisers, not expressions of the centre itself. It does not belong to either side. It transmits stabilising constraint symmetrically.

Enables longevity of the pyramids across future generations.

Mapping Pattern to the Site

The pyramids demonstrate high precision in placement and measurements. It integrates alignment with cardinal directions, stellar alignment (with Orion constellation as at 10,500 BC), and human processional routes. This is systems level planning.

The pattern suggests this is a carefully designed system, meant to stabilise, harmonise, and anchor the balance of left / centre / right. At a moment in time when they were perfectly balanced. Intention being to preserve this balance into the future.

— —

Pattern Reading 2 — The Sphinx

Shape sensed:
Off-centre right: Grounded dome

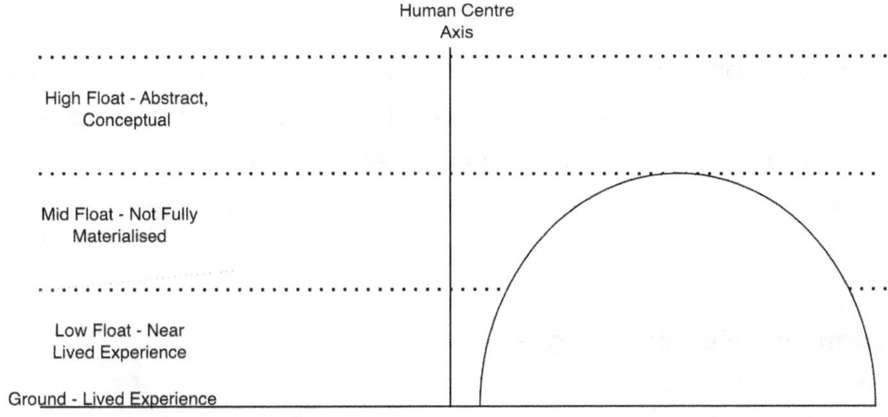

Pattern Interpretation

A dome implies containment, sheltering, and holding.
Off-centre right is orientation towards authority, structure, abstraction.
Grounded means embedded in land.

Unlike the pyramids, the Sphinx does not transmit orientation. It holds and protects an already stabilised system.

Mapping Pattern to the Site

The Great Sphinx is the guardian of the pyramid system. It is carved from the bedrock of the area, inferring it stabilises the site using the existing environment. A lion's body has the attributes of instinct and presence. And a human head has the attributes of awareness and cognition.

Its orientation is in line with astronomical alignments, like the sun setting between the Sphinx and Khafre's pyramid during equinoxes, suggesting intentional system design.

— —

Combined Reading — Pyramids + Sphinx

The pyramids and Sphinx represent a period where left, centre, right capacities were simultaneously active. They do not represent the start of a civilisation, but a rare period of equilibrium that was intended to be anchored and protected.

Afterwards, over time, left side capacities diminished, right side systems expanded. The balance shifted from integration to control. Later built ancient pyramids around the world show comparatively less technical achievement. They mimic the form, but lack integrated function.

Avebury Stone Circle

The Avebury Stone Circle is located in Wiltshire, England. It is a massive circle 330 metres in diameter, comprised of arranged sarsen stones, some weighing up to 50 tonnes, and over 5 metres tall. Inside the circle are two smaller circles and processional avenues. The stones' characteristics are irregular shapes and varied sizes.

There is a focal point in the north part of the circle, called the Cove which consists of two massive stones (originally three in a U shape). Another focal point that was there, was the Obelisk in the south part of the circle.

Avebury's construction date was estimated to be 3000 BC, and used over many centuries. The Avebury Village grew inside the perimeter of the circle by 9th century AD.

There is no clear function of the circle, which is likely broader than ritual gathering. It appears to be a relational site with processional avenues leading to other nearby places.

— —

Pattern Reading

The shapes are read relationally, with orientation, effort, and authority relative to a human centre centre axis.

Shapes Sensed
- Off-centre right: Straight vertical line with slight right tilt (~10°)
- Off-centre left: Tall, solid pillar. Grounded and near centre axis

— —

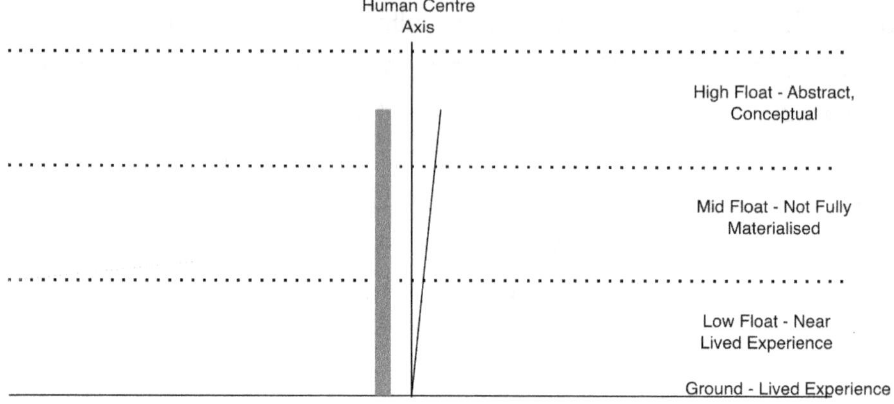

Pattern Interpretation

General insight:

The co-presence of two vertical elements (left and right), both grounded and unfaded, distinguishes this pattern from the compensatory and preservation-based structures covered in previous chapters.
This indicates it's a fully balanced and coherent structure. Not a dominant structure.

Off-centre right: Straight vertical line with slight right tilt (~10°)

Right side symbolises order, continuity, and effort.
The slight tilt represents orientation towards structure, coordination and abstraction.
Grounded and unfaded means functional right-side systems.

Off-centre left: Tall, solid pillar. Grounded and near centre axis

Left side represents distributed orientation.

It being a tall pillar, grounded and near the centre axis shows a strong relational coherence with humans. Normalising the availability of distributed knowing within everyday life.

It's solid, meaning the left side capacity is fully active.

— —

Mapping Pattern to the Site

The integration with daily life of people in Avebury Village demonstrates coherence embedded in activity. No dismantling and minimal damage to the stone over centuries of habitation.

The Cove at Avebury was partially enclosed, inward shaped (U shape), and not visually dominant from afar. Symbolically it signifies containment, listening, anchoring and holding. It is not a command centre but a settling basin for coherence. A place where orientation settles rather than where meaning is imposed. In the past, people likely arrived here to be in alignment.

Avebury reflects lived orientation rather than preservation or compensation. The open design of the stone circle allows choice, movement and continuity. There is internal coherence present. The stone echo and amplify the coherence. It is not a teaching structure. Externalisation of orientation was not necessary, unlike Labyrinth of Hawara. The internal relational knowing of the building culture was sufficient at the time.

Such coherence appears to require stable conditions across generations, something that would not persist indefinitely. This is a rare example in today's age, of left and right sides functioning together.

Conclusion: Ancient Sites

There are ancient sites dotted around the world, that tease us with inconsistencies and seemingly illogical approaches, compared to our understanding of history.

Relational reading reveals patterns of human orientation, showing how knowledge, authority, and coherence were distributed relative to the human centre. This is not belief. This is not theoretical.

We are familiar with the right side orientation, being key primary attributes of humanity as we know it. Abstraction, structure, hierarchy, formalised effort. It works by isolating, measuring, and manipulating discrete objects and variables.

The centre is human coherence, embodiment, and lived continuity. It integrates and mediates experience.

Left side orientation senses relational, distributed patterns, and coherence across non-localised systems. Information exists between elements and is not isolated. This is the basis for "distributed orientation", defined as human capacity to allow all information, especially left-side, to be sensed without prematurely collapsing it in abstraction, integrating left and right side knowing. In plain language, is it access to relational and systematic awareness without forcing it into abstraction.

The sites discussed in this section show which capacities were intact, weakening, externalised, compensating, preserved, or lost. They are not a random collection. But show a range of strategies to cope with fading distributed orientation.

The patterns across the sites discussed:
• Gobekli Tepe – Left-side still present but weakening. Right-side effort compensates.
• Easter Island Statues – Right-side compensates for fading left-side through externalised reminders.
• Labyrinth of Hawara – Left-side no longer reliable and is encoded externally.
• Derinkuyu – Left-side survives in a protected cohort, sheltered and hidden to preserve a human way of being.
• Giza Pyramids & Sphinx – Stabilisation by a civilisation capable of holding left, centre, right simultaneously in equilibrium.
• Avebury Stones – Left-side orientation intact and normal. No compensation, preservation, or central authority demonstrated. The site survived in coherence despite humanity having lost distributed orientation as a dominant mode.

The overall trend is of the left-side fading, gradually and unevenly, across a time period, whilst the right-side compensates and eventually continues functioning without it.

A quick read on the pattern of humanity today shows a centred tree with dense branching mostly on the right. It is what is absent that is the most telling. No noticeable branching on the left and centre. The human centre is increasingly burdened mediating without left-side support. Resulting in modern humans being imbalanced (but not broken). The well developed right side masks loss of left side, with consequences surfacing indirectly as fragmentation, disconnection, anxiety, ecological instability, and need for external coherence regulation.

Interpretations we are accustomed to, rely on a dominant right-side perspective with tools, beliefs, and construction methods. This creates a bias relative to original human orientation. The aim of this book is to highlight what was forgotten, how the forgetting occurred, what replaced it, without claiming restoration.

And we will also use the original human orientation as a lens to view Earth's other mysteries, which will give a layer of insight which may be simpler than we think, but also surprising.

Next section looks at how humanity forgot the left side, and what happens when a civilisation outgrows one mode of knowing before fully understanding what was replaced. This will set the stage for analysing modern anomalies and mysteries through the left / centre / right lens.

How Humans Lost Distributed Orientation

Younger Dryas

If ancient sites show how humanity responded to fading distributed orientation, the Younger Dryas may reveal why that fading began.

There was a period of abrupt climate instability about 12 to 13 thousand years ago, called the Younger Dryas. Often associated with sharp temperature drop, fractured seasonal patterns, landscape transformations such as advancing ice, shifting coastlines and erratic rainfall. With resulting food source fluctuations, this put survival as a priority for civilisation at that time.

Human life before the Younger Dryas had relatively stable ecological rhythms. When the climate instability happened, it was a shock to orientation, not just survival.

The pattern readings for human perception before and after the Younger Dryas are presented below.

——

Pattern of before the Younger Dryas: Short tree stump in centre axis, with interweaving roots running across ground on the left.

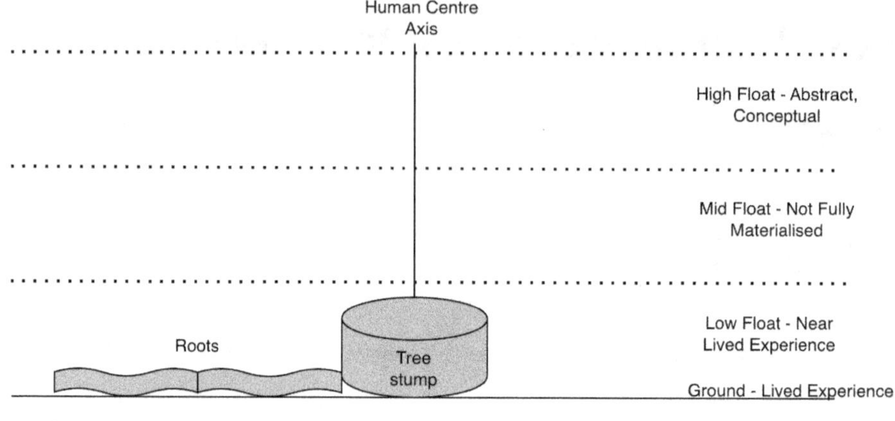

Symbolically, this is a classic image of low vertical differentiation, not a hierarchical society. With high horizontal integration represented by the interwoven roots spreading across the left. Orientation is embedded in the land, kin, and ecology. Knowledge is relationally stored (as an idea, a possible example is the patterns sensed and presented in this book).

Humanity wasn't "advanced upward" in a technological sense, but it was deeply networked sideways. That aligns with distributed orientation, harmonic relationships with landscapes, sensory as primary with abstraction less emphasised, high relational coherence. This is a stable configuration, not a primitive one.

— —

Pattern of after the Younger Dryas: Tall tree on centre axis with right-side branching at the top. No noticeable left or centre branching.

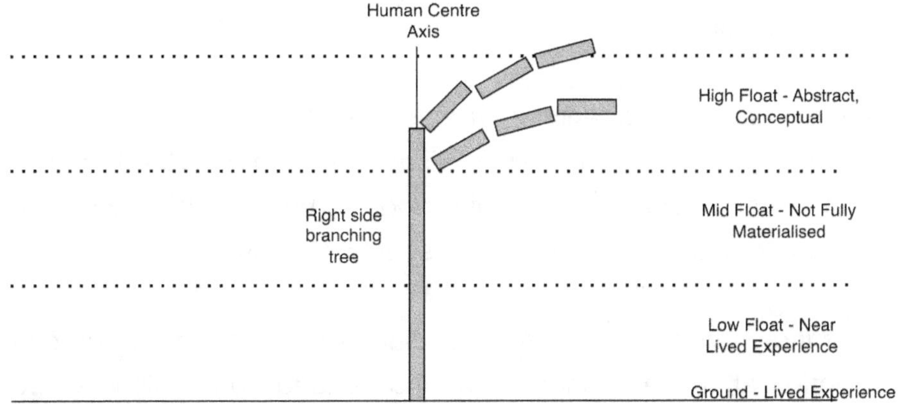

This represents vertical growth, associated with hierarchy, abstraction, and cumulative systems. The late branching implies delayed introduction of right side attributes (analysis, control, hierarchy, formal knowledge), possibly due to being forced to develop it for survival. The tree stump having evolved to tree trunk indicates an increase in vertical organisation under pressure, not an increase in coherence.

— —

Humanity survived by growing "upward and outward" cognitively, but lost sideways integration. Society shifted to agriculture, settlements, hierarchy, law, formal knowledge transmission. Right-side orientation became primary, because it was adaptable, and importantly, scalable as population grew.

Left-side orientation works best under stable conditions. Distributed orientation depends on continuity of relational signals across time; volatility fragments those signals. Right-side capacities become more effective under volatility. The Younger Dryas created conditions under which distributed orientation could no longer be reliably maintained.

Nothing "broke" suddenly. Left-side orientation slowly became situational, localised, and specialised, as demonstrated in the ancient sites discussed in this book. The left-side was not deliberately forgotten or lost. It was simply outgrown.

Interestingly, when a pattern reading was applied to human perception after the Younger Dryas had ended—once climate and land had stabilised—it produced no distinct configuration. This absence is itself meaningful. Symbolically, it suggests the Younger Dryas did not conclude in a way that re-oriented human perception once environmental stability returned. There was no renewed configuration of knowing. Instead, orientation appears to have remained organised around survival.

This points to a civilisational trauma response.

The crisis resolved environmentally, but not perceptually.

Distributed orientation did not re-establish itself. What followed was not recovery, but adaptation.

In this light, the megalithic monuments, mythic structures, and early institutions that appear afterward can be understood as workarounds—external supports developed during a prolonged transition from left-side distributed orientation to right-side abstraction and control. They are not expressions of restored coherence, but compensatory structures built in its absence.

Humanity survived the Younger Dryas, but it did not fully remember itself afterward.

In the next chapter, we will pattern-read the Great Flood.

Different cultures around the world have a flood myth narrative. It likely is a narrative compression of prolonged disruption to human life. It does not require a literal global flood. It is a symbolic representation of total loss of orientation, resulting in no stable ground, and preservation of a select few (survival ark analogies). The purpose of the myth is to document human experience of disrupted orientation.

The Great Flood

Flood stories appear globally—in Mesopotamia, India, the Americas, and elsewhere. Across cultures, recurring elements are consistent: rising waters, loss of stable ground, collapse of familiar systems, and preservation of fragments to allow continuity.

Debate continues as to whether these floods were local or global, singular or repeated, geological events or purely mythical. The relational pattern reading in this chapter indicates that the Great Flood represents overwhelmed human orientation. The flood functions as an abstraction for the loss of reliable reference, not merely an excess of water.

— —

Pattern Reading

The left / centre / right axis remains applicable for relational reading of an event. For large-scale destabilising events, right-side qualities — interpretation, abstraction, control attempts, and explanatory pressure — become dominant.

Shapes sensed:
- Off-centre right: Mid-height, floating logarithmic curve
- Middle right: Grounded, small, faded square

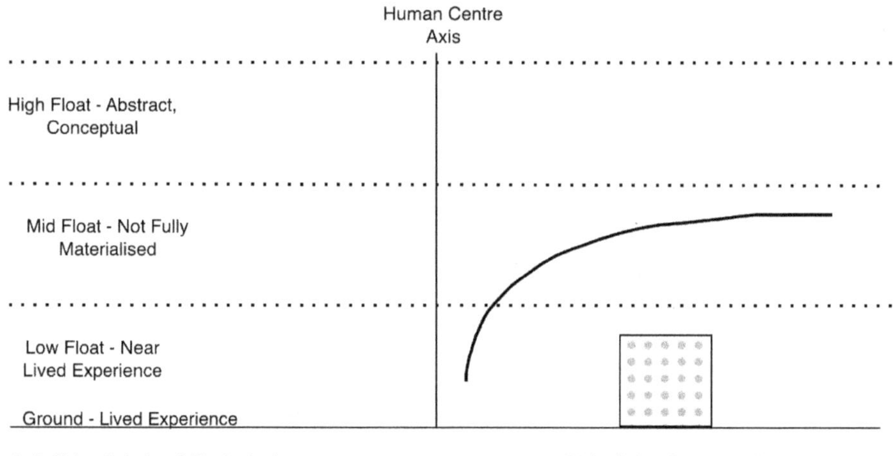

— —

Pattern Interpretation

Off-centre right: Mid-height, floating logarithmic curve

A logarithmic curve represents escalation that accelerates faster than adaptation, followed by saturation.

Floating indicates severed continuity with land, rhythm, and inherited orientation.

Mid-height suggests humans are still alive, thinking, reacting, and attempting to interpret events, but unable to stabilise meaning. Perception cannot resolve what is happening in real time. This is precisely the perceptual territory where myth forms.

Middle right: Grounded, small, faded square

A square represents structure, containment, and order.
Faded indicates reduced vitality relative to the original coherence it attempts to preserve.
Small suggests limited scope — a fragment rather than a whole.
Grounded implies practical survival value rather than symbolic or relational completeness.

——

Mapping Pattern to the Flood Narrative

This pattern maps cleanly to flood narratives across cultures: rapid onset of chaos, loss of familiar landmarks and rhythms, survival through containment or rule, minimal viable order preserved, and eventual emergence into a changed world once escalation saturates and stabilises.

The square, expressed mythologically as the ark, preserves continuity but does not restore distributed orientation. Flood myths frequently conclude not with restoration of relational knowing, but with new laws, covenants, hierarchies, boundaries, and moral codes. The flood marks the narrative threshold where lived coherence can no longer regenerate itself internally.

The transition from flood to post-flood civilisation represents a departure from distributed orientation and the emergence of right-side systems designed to manage coherence externally: law, hierarchy, formalised authority, and structured knowledge transmission. This shift is adaptive rather than regressive. Right-side systems are essential for survival under unstable conditions, and are scalable as populations grow.

The Great Flood, read relationally, is not a story about destruction alone. It is a record of the moment humanity crossed from lived coherence, into system-managed coherence.

Living Inside the Right-sided Tree

The right-sided tree pattern that appears after the Younger Dryas is not yet the world we live in. It is the structural form that made the modern world possible. To understand how this structure behaves once embedded in daily life, we need to return to it from within lived experience.

After the Great Flood threshold, humanity reorganised how knowing and perception operate. Intelligence remained intact, but orientation shifted. Knowing moved from lived perception to structured interpretation.

Revisiting the right-sided tree pattern of humanity after the flood:

• Tall, centred vertical trunk
• Dense branching canopy
• Branching almost entirely on the right

• No noticeable branching on the left and centre

The trunk represents continuity of civilisation. The structure is stable, not broken. Growth succeeded through a prolonged period of instability, but it was asymmetrical. Orientation became dominated by right-side capacities: structure, abstraction, and systematisation.

The dense right-side canopy represents the proliferation of disciplines, institutions, technologies, external records, theories, and models. Complexity scales and accumulates. Knowledge no longer needs to be lived to persist; it survives through recording, teaching, and enforcement. Coherence becomes externalised, allowing civilisation to accelerate without requiring relational feedback at every level.

The centre shows little or no branching. The human centre functions primarily as a mediator. The asymmetrical shape suggests humans are increasingly burdened by abstraction, expanding systems, and multiplying demands. The centre bears load rather than developing capacity. This helps explain modern experiences of overwhelm, anxiety, fragmentation, and overstimulation. This is compensation, not collapse.

As time passed after the Younger Dryas, left-side functions were progressively replaced by right-side structures:

Religion replaced meaning through direct perception:
Religion functions as stored orientation, stabilising meaning when lived coherence fades. Doctrine replaces shared relational knowing. Authority replaces communal attunement. This is an adaptive response, not deception.

Science replaced knowledge through embodiment:
Science stabilises predictive accuracy rather than meaning. Measurement replaces perception. Instruments replace sensing. Repeatability replaces lived feedback. This increases reliability and scale, but removes the knower from the known. Relational context is reduced.

Theoretical models replaced understanding through intuition:
Models engage systems too complex to perceive directly by simplifying, abstracting, and predicting. Models are not living fields and lack relational context. Intuition becomes distrusted—not because it is false, but because it is non-portable and non-verifiable at scale.

Peer review replaced consensus through sensing:
Validation through shared presence and relational feedback is replaced by methodological agreement, institutional legitimacy, and statistical thresholds. Truth becomes what survives scrutiny, rather than what resonates relationally.

Interpretation replaced perception:
Interpretation becomes the primary mode of knowing. When perception lacks reliable orientation, the human mind supplies symbolic containers. Experience is shaped to be communicable, defensible, and rememberable.

The Structure of Human Perception

Carl Jung, the psychotherapist, proposed that symbols arise from cultural and mythic structures rather than being arbitrary. This is directionally correct, but incomplete. Symbols are not the originating interface, nor are they simply imagery. They are compensatory outputs that appear when direct perception is no longer fully available.

Different eras produce different symbolic containers. Unexplained airships, flying saucers, drones, gods, demons, angels, orbs, and aliens all function as stabilising forms for perception within a given cultural context. The container, however, is not the underlying phenomenon.

This distinction is central to understanding how human perception has changed.

— —

Left-Side Perception Sequencing

Cultures with intact distributed orientation typically follow this perceptual sequence:

1. Direct relational sensing
This is pre-form, pre-symbol, pre-explanation. The world is encountered as field, presence, pressure, resonance, absence, and change. Meaning is sensed before it is named.

2. Shared coherence across people and land
Orientation is continuously corrected through relationship with landscape, ecology, repetition, and consequence. Meaning is not privately owned. It is distributed and mutually regulated.

3. Narrative as memory, not reality
Story, image, taboo, and being arise after perception. They function as mnemonic anchors, teaching devices, orientation reminders, and compressions for transmission.

A mythic being emerges at step three. No one encounters the mythic being at step one. The symbol is not mistaken for the field. The being exists to re-open sensing, not to replace it.

(In this book when talking about perception in context of the left-side, it does not mean interpretation, visual imagery, belief, or mental representation. It refers to direct relational sensing - the capacity to register coherence, pressure, absence, alignment, and change before those impressions are shaped into symbols, stories, or explanations. This mode of perception is pre-conceptual and non-symbolic. It is not something one "thinks", but something one is oriented within. Meaning arises from participation, not observation.)

— —

Modern Perception Sequencing

Modern civilisation typically follows the reverse order:

1. Narrative arrives first
Story, belief, entity, and explanation are prioritised.

2. Perception is recruited to support the narrative
Observations are selected, interpreted, or emphasised to stabilise the story.

3. Shared coherence never forms

Meaning becomes individual, ideological, or institutional rather than relational.

This reversal explains why unidentified aerial phenomena harden into aliens, gods harden into authorities, myths harden into dogma, and symbols harden into ontology.

The core error is mistaking step three for step one. Meaning was once lived first and narrated second. Much modern confusion arises from narrating first and attempting to live inside the story.

(Author's note: The shapes used in this book are intended as the closest modern analogue to step one — direct relational sensing — without collapsing into imagery or belief.)

— —

A Note on Science

Science explicitly recognises the risks of premature narration and compensates for them by delaying interpretation.
1. Data is gathered before meaning is assigned
2. Interpretation is formalised and constrained
3. Consensus is sought only after review and replication

Science functions best when:
• The observed system is stable
• The phenomenon does not change under observation
• Repetition is possible
• The observer does not meaningfully affect the outcome

Distributed orientation operates precisely where these conditions break down.

Phenomena involving attention, meaning, relational context, and observer participation cannot be fully stabilised by data alone. This is not a flaw in science. It is a boundary condition.

When the perceptual organ is removed, coherence must be negotiated rather than felt. Consensus replaces shared sensing. Peer review replaces communal attunement. Agreement replaces resonance. The structure remains. The organ is gone.

Many modern anomalies arise along this fault line — where perception weakened, narrative took precedence, and symbolic containers were mistaken for the phenomena they once pointed toward.

Mythic Beings

Aborigine Cave Art — Wandjina

In Aboriginal Australian Dreaming, the Wandjina are creator beings and rain-making presences. They are central to the spiritual and cultural life of certain Aboriginal communities. To these cultures, Wandjina are not myths in the modern sense. They are the forces that shaped the landscape, established law, and continue to regulate weather, seasons, and continuity of life.

Western interpretation typically classifies the Wandjina as deities, ancestors, or supernatural beings. These categories collapse their function into belief-based ontology and miss the perceptual role they serve within the original human orientation.

The Wandjina are among the most recognisable figures in Aboriginal cave art. Their depiction is highly consistent and symbolically precise. They are almost always shown without a mouth, with large black eyes, white bodies, and halo-like headdresses.

Unlike most ancient cave art, Wandjina imagery belongs to a living tradition. The paintings are periodically refreshed and repainted by traditional custodians. This is not restoration of an artefact. It is renewal of relationship.

——

Pattern Reading of Wandjina Cave Painting
• Long, solid oval

- Vertical
- Centred on the human axis, slightly offset to the right

Pattern Interpretation and Mapping

The oval indicates a container rather than a narrative or structure. It is a holding form. Its vertical extension implies duration and continuity rather than a discrete event. Solidity indicates reliability — a form returned to repeatedly over time. Placement near the human axis ties this presence directly to lived orientation and daily continuity.

This pattern maps to a cloud-being or weather-law custodian. Not a personality, and not an entity in the modern sense, but a stabilising presence that holds coherence across seasonal cycles, rainfall patterns, flood memory, and moral law as encoded in land and weather.

The slight rightward offset indicates partial externalisation for transmission. The presence is shared, maintained, and taught, but not abstracted into doctrine or belief. It remains relational rather than conceptual.

The visual features of the Wandjina follow directly from this function.

The black eyes represent awareness that blankets a landscape rather than localised vision.
The absence of a mouth reflects that they do not speak — they are weather.
The halo-like headdress corresponds to a condensation or atmospheric field.

The art is not depicting a face. It is depicting the shape of a presence using the available visual grammar.

In this sense, the Wandjina are not humanoid spirits. They are climate beings.

This is narrative as memory, not narrative as reality. The Wandjina arise after perception, not before it. They function as perceptual stabilisers rather than literal entities. Their role is to maintain relational sensing between humans and environmental forces.

Within Aboriginal Dreaming, the Wandjina operate as custodians of atmospheric order, keepers of seasonal law, and memory nodes for land–weather reciprocity. They are not ancestors. They are senior Dreaming infrastructure — systems already operating before human arrival.

Repainting the Wandjina renews perceptual alignment. The practice maintains orientation and relationship, not belief.

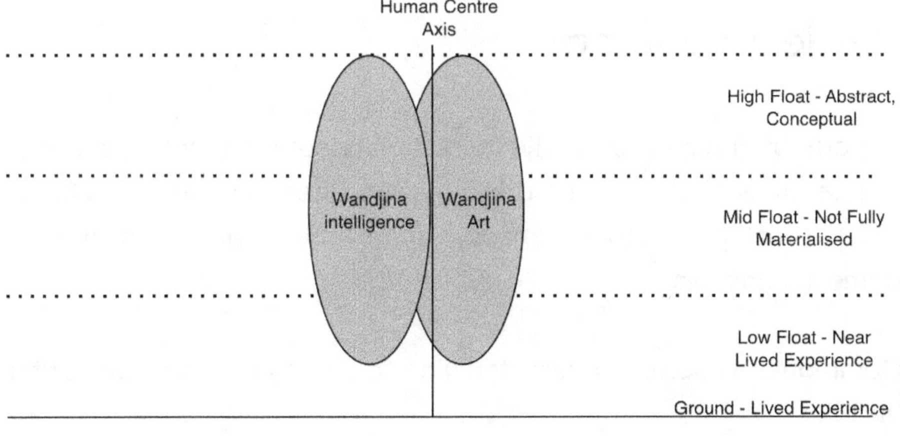

— —

Pattern Reading of Wandjina Intelligence
- Long, solid oval
- Vertical
- Floating on left side
- Touching the centre

Pattern Interpretation and Mapping

This pattern confirms that the intelligence the Wandjina relate to is fundamentally left-sided and distributed, as a weather system would be. And the form appears near the human axis because the cave art records the interface, not the source. The fact that the recorded shape of the long solid oval maps to the intelligence itself shows how left-side culture preserved perception without collapsing it into belief or doctrine. Ancient cultures did not mistake interfaces for intelligences. Modern cultures do.

Cattle Mutilation

Reports of unexplained cattle mutilation occur worldwide. The term "cattle mutilation" is an umbrella, as the phenomenon also affects other livestock—horses, sheep, goats, pigs—and occasionally domestic animals.

Commonly reported characteristics of a mutilation encounter include:

- Precise excisions: Removal of specific organs, most often eyes, tongue, ears, jaw flesh, genitals, and rectum. Incisions are frequently described as surgically clean.
- Exsanguination: The carcass appears drained of blood, with little or no pooling on the ground.
- Absence of tracks: No footprints, tire marks, or scavenger trails are found near the body.
- Healthy targets: Animals affected are often the healthiest in the herd, rather than the weak or old typically targeted by predators.

Conventional explanations—predation, human activity, hoaxes, extraterrestrial intervention—each account for fragments, but not the pattern as a whole. The consistency across geography and time suggests a structured interaction rather than random violence.

This book does not approach cattle mutilation as a forensic crime to be solved. It approaches it as a patterned interaction between animals, land, humans, and non-human intelligences.

——

Pattern Reading

Shape 1
A crescent-moon curve, open toward the left. The human centre axis bisects the curve. The lower arc is grounded on the left.

Shape 2
A floating D-shape touching the centre axis.

——

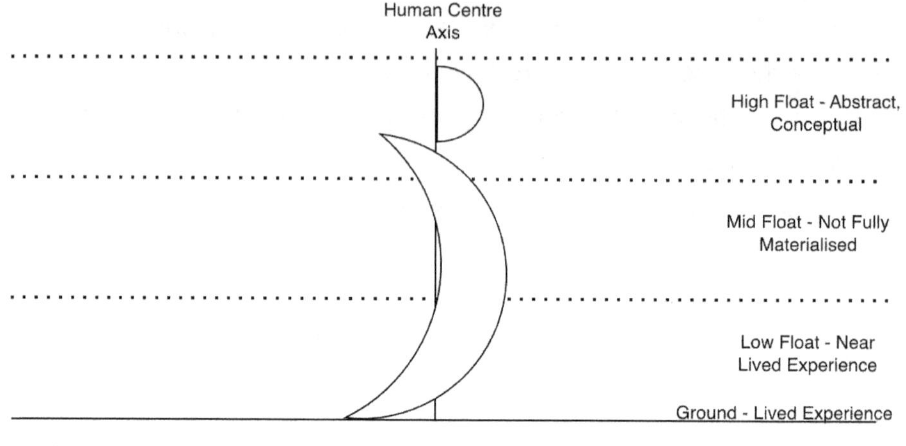

Pattern Interpretation and Mapping

The crescent curve, open to the left, indicates partial interface rather than embodied presence. The presence engages relational fields but does not integrate with them. The curve's belly sits on the right, with extension into the left, suggesting functional engagement without participation in relational continuity.

The grounded left base indicates a land-based, ecological presence. It is place-bound rather than abstract, technological, or "visitation"-oriented. Its activity is tied to terrain, conditions, or environmental thresholds rather than intention or communication.

The human centre axis bisecting the curve shows repeated intersection with human and animal life, but without stabilisation or residency. The interaction passes through the field rather than settling within it. This maps directly to the nature of the mutilations: discrete, repeatable interactions with no escalation, warning, or aftermath.

The floating D-shape touching the centre axis clarifies the mode of engagement. Its floating position indicates liminal timing rather than continuous presence. Contact with biological systems is selective and limited. There is no reciprocal relationship, no signalling, and no attempt at continuity.

The focus on sensory organs, reproductive tissue, and signalling systems suggests sampling, calibration, or maintenance, rather than predation or ritualised violence. From a relational lens, the activity is indifferent to narrative meaning.

This presence differs from the Wandjina. Left-side relational presences are readily mythologised. Right-side presences tend to be distorted through abstraction. This presence operates across both domains without belonging fully to either, making it particularly resistant to stable mythic representation.

A composite description of the intelligence:
- Non-relational
- Non-communicative
- Ecologically based
- Does not seek recognition, worship, or explanation
- Engages biological systems directly
- Leaves minimal symbolic residue
- Functional rather than expressive
- Difficult to mythologise without distortion

In cultures with distributed orientation, such a presence would not have been investigated or explained. Instead, its activity would have been contained through land practice: marking places as unsafe, establishing taboos, adjusting herd movement, timing, or land use.

If mythologised at all, it would likely appear as a life-taker or bone-thief associated with livestock, liminal hours, and boundary zones. Figures that loosely map to this category include El Silbón (Colombia and Venezuela) and the Kasha (Japan).

Modern culture demands explanation and narrative closure. Non-relational phenomena resist this demand. When explanation fails, the phenomenon collapses into aliens, secret experiments, or fear-based speculation.

Cattle mutilation does not suggest a new intelligence. It suggests a familiar one encountered by a culture that no longer knows how to hold it without forcing narrative collapse.

Nephthys

In Egyptian mythology, Nephthys is associated with death, mourning, night, and the threshold between worlds. She is Isis' quieter sister, often positioned in shadow and peripheral roles. Modern interpretations tend to treat her as secondary, passive, or symbolic. This framing misses her function.

Nephthys is not a teacher, not a judge, and not a figure of destination. Her domain is transition. She appears where form is dissolving and meaning has not yet reassembled. She stands at the edge of what is ending and ensures that nothing essential is prematurely lost or falsely resolved.

She does not guide the living forward, nor does she govern what comes next. She attends the interval itself.

— —

Pattern Reading

- Off-centre left
- Grounded
- A curve like the left half of a large circle

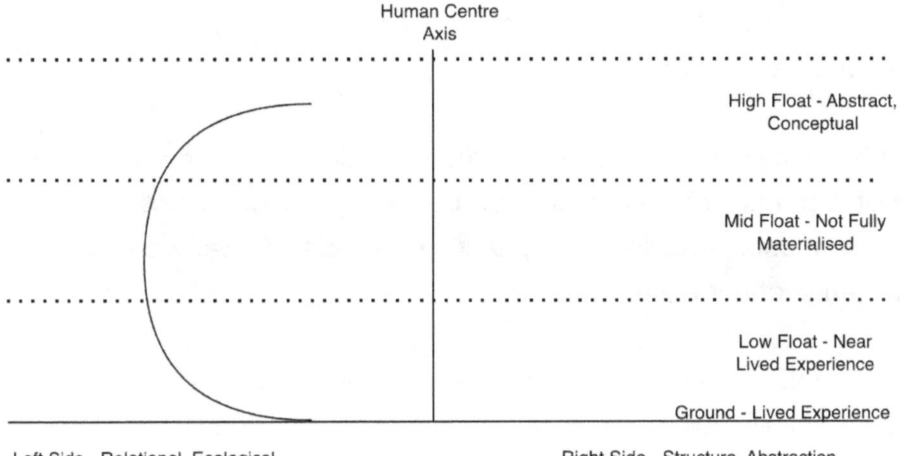

— —

Pattern Interpretation and Mapping

Left-side placement indicates that Nephthys operates relationally, without authority or command. Her presence is not instructional. It does not impose order. It does not conclude.

The half-circle is a receiving form without enclosure. It holds without sealing. There is no containment, no resolution, and no closure. This maps directly to her domain: the phase where something has ended, but nothing new should yet be named.

59

Because the curve is grounded, Nephthys does not operate in transcendence. She works at the incarnate level — with bodies, land, time, decay, grief, and endings. In relation to death, her concern is not the afterlife as a destination, but the passage itself. She attends the interval between coherence and reconfiguration.

Her function is presence without intervention. She does not repair, accelerate, or transform. She prevents premature reassembly of meaning. She allows dissolution to complete without collapse. What should pass is allowed to pass. What must remain is not stripped away by haste.

This is why Nephthys is associated with silence, shadow, and night. Not because she is dark, but because she does not interrupt. Speech could stabilise. Explanation could distort. Her work requires absence of narrative pressure.

In Egyptian myth, Nephthys presides over mourning and burial rites. She establishes the boundary around what has ended. She is present when form has expired but transition is incomplete. She is often paired with her sister Isis. Isis reassembles. Nephthys ensures the timing is correct. Restoration depends on waiting. Reconstitution depends on allowing disintegration to finish its work.

Modern culture rushes transition. It demands explanation, reframing, lessons, and meaning extraction. These are right-side compensations for discomfort with unheld intervals. When her function is no longer lived, Nephthys is mythologised into a goddess of darkness or death. In truth, she is neither.

She is the condition that allows endings to remain clean.

Totemic Animals

The practice of identifying with a totemic animal as a spiritual ancestor or clan protector is a near global phenomenon. North American indigenous culture had a society organised into totemic animal clans. Australian Aboriginal culture had individuals linked to totemic animals. Siberian and North Asian cultures intertwine totemic relationships with shamanism.

Totemic animals are not animal mascots. They are orientation interfaces between humans, land, and specific behavioural intelligences. The animal form is not the source of power. It is the shape through which coherence is held and transmitted.

——

Pattern Reading — Totemic Animals as a Whole

Shape: Off-centre left. Medium sized solid circle. Grounded.

Pattern Interpretation and Mapping

Being on the left-side, totemic animals are relational and non-authoritative. A circle represents containment without hierarchy and inherently whole. Grounded is embedded in land, ecology, and lived behaviour. And that it is solid, access is reliable and repeatable over time.

Totemic animals function as everyday life orientation anchors. They are not transcendent beings or rulers. And are not aspirational metaphors (ie. "brave like a lion"). They are meant to stabilise the cultures' relationships and return them to a complete relational behavioural mode. There are many stable patterns of behavioural modes, represented by the different totemic animals.

Totemic knowledge was lived through hunting, seasonal movements of the culture, conflict, parenting, survival, and guided situations when not to act, where not to go, how long to wait, and how to withdraw without collapse of coherence. It reduced the need for abstract rules by embedding behaviour in relationships.

— —

Specific Totem Examples

Wolf Totem

Shape: Off-centre left. Grounded vertical line. Tilted slightly to the left by about 10 degrees.

The vertical line indicates continuity, endurance, lineage transmission across generations. Being grounded, it is lived, practical and ecological. The leftward tilt prioritises relational coordination over individual dominance.

This maps to the group coherence of wolves. Ecological awareness, coordinated movement through unstable terrain, distributed decision making. It is not about aggression or hierarchy. Wolf totems stabilise how groups move together without central command.

Eagle Totem

Shape: Off-centre left. Floating curve like a "smile".

This is a relational awareness without control totem. The curve and that it is floating relative to the horizontal axis, indicates a wide perceptual view of the land.

The Eagle totem governs pattern recognition, timing, and long range situational awareness. It watches till conditions align for action. The Eagle does not act first, allowing perception to widen without disassociation. Eagle totems appear where cultures need overview without control — to see without collapsing what is seen.

Bear Totem

Shape: Off-centre left. Grounded vertical line. Tilted slightly to the right. About 10 degrees.

Vertical means endurance and continuity. And grounded brings qualities of body and metabolic embodiment and living with seasonal rhythm. It reflects deep embodiment. The bear does not leave the world to see it. It sinks into it. Slight right tilt is engagement with effort and force, but still relationally anchored given it's on the left-side.

The Bear governs boundary enforcement, regeneration through stillness and coherence, and defines when inaction is correct action. In human terms, it allows things to be paused without loss of status. It protects the human centre from burning out. But there is action when needed for boundary enforcement.

—

Compared to Wandjina and Nephthys, Totemic Animals are situational and activated through behaviour. They are lived and do not require belief. Mythic beings arise later as narrative containers. As left-side distributed orientation weakened, totems lost their relational connection and became symbols. And symbols became archetypes and personal identity markers. Modern "spirit animals" retain the image, but not the relational function. What was once land-tied and collective, became psychological and portable.

Cryptids

Mermaids

In maritime history around the world, there are persistent legends around sightings of beautiful women whose lower bodies are that of a fish - mermaids. An example is that of Christopher Columbus when he was sailing in 1493. While exploring the Caribbean, Columbus documented seeing three mermaids. Modern historians believe he was actually seeing manatees or dugongs, which have front flippers and can rise out of the water in a way that vaguely resembles a human torso from a distance.

To superstitious sailors, mermaids were often bad omens. A sighting was often associated with an impending storm, or a shipwreck. This led to the tradition of carved wooden women on the prows of ship meant to appease the sea and guarantee safe passage.

Modern explanations from the lenses of myth, fantasy, and misidentified animals, miss seeing its functional role.

— —

Pattern Reading

Shape: Off-centre left. Tall vertical line, curving left near the top 30 degrees relative to vertical axis.

— —

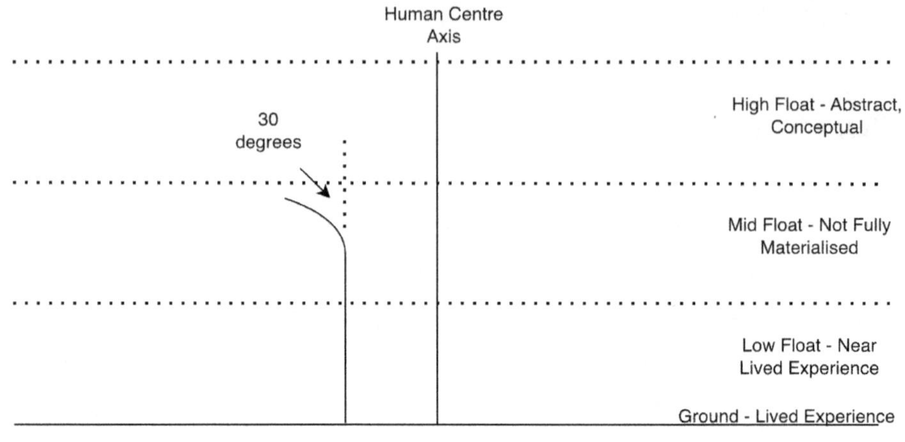

Pattern Interpretation and Mapping

Left side places mermaids in the relational, non-authoritative and non-hierarchal type phenomenon. Tall vertical line represents continuity and repeated encounters over long periods of time. Together with being grounded, it also represents the embodied human upright orientation, but it's carried into the left non-human domain.

The leftward curve near the top is the crux of this phenomenon. It shows relational perception bending under strain after a long period of time, but not collapsing. Perception is pulled sideways away from coherence, under conditions of fatigue of unending water view, isolation, and potential danger.

Open water of the sea removes stable reference points. With the horizon being the only thing visible for days on end, the glare of the sun on water, fog under some climate conditions, the rhythmic motion of the sea, all serve to disrupt orientation. Humans on ships serve long vigilance in between lands under such circumstances. Perception is stretched beyond its stable operating range.

Mermaids are not aquatic beings from an undersea civilisation. Nor are they cryptozoological animals. They arise from relational perception under environmental stress. They are perceptual subjects formed at the boundary where human orientation fails when in open waters.

Why did sailors see the mermaid form? Half human, half fish. Mermaids are consistently depicted as partially human because perception does not fully externalise. Unlike some cryptos and aliens where the phenomena collapses under observation and hardens fully into an "other". Human upper body symbolises continuity of the human self-recognition. The observer still knows this relates to him. The fish tail symbolises environmental otherness. Movement, breath and survival in a domain where humans cannot survive unaided. The seam between human and fish marks the exact boundary where land-based orientation fails.

Mermaids are not hybrids in terms of biology, but hybrids in the perception applied to them.

Why are they females? Within the perceptual grammar of the observing culture, females reflect the cultural expectation of relational perception. Attraction without ownership. Relating without containing. These qualities are softer in nature.

In comparison to animal totems, totems stabilise behaviour within habitable environments. When distributed orientation weakens, the warning of weakening orientation is no longer felt directly. It collapses into narration. The pattern externalises. Narrative replaced lived calibration.

What did mermaids warn against? The warning is this: "You are no longer moving by lived orientation." In left-side society times, this means the sea is no longer felt. That was when ships run aground as weather was misjudged, or the ship was was into conditions they should have waited out. That was why superstitious sailors thought mermaids were often bad omens.

In left-side societies, distributed orientation does not make someone immune to environmental strain. But it does make them immune to hallucinated ontology. They would say something like: "The water is unreadable" or "The timing is wrong." Not: "There is a woman in the water."

Modern maritime culture has instruments, maps, engines, and protocols. The relational interface with the sea has been largely substituted. As a result, mermaids no longer arise warnings. They survive as stories, fantasies, and entertainment devoid of function.

Bigfoot

Long before the term "Bigfoot" entered modern popular culture, Indigenous peoples across North America had stories of "wild people" of the forests and mountains. In many traditions, these beings were not animals in the ordinary sense. They were described as another kind of people, or as non-human intelligences associated with wilderness, thresholds, and ecological order. Some were regarded as custodians of remote land.

The most famous modern evidence is the Patterson–Gimlin footage filmed in 1967 at Bluff Creek, California. The film shows a large, upright, hair-covered biped walking across a clearing and briefly turning its head toward the camera. Skeptics argue it depicts a man in a costume. Others have noted that the gait, limb proportions, and visible muscle movement would have been difficult to fabricate convincingly with known costume technology of the period.

Despite decades of sightings, no confirmed body, skeleton, or settlement evidence has been recovered. Contemporary explanations tend to polarise between undiscovered hominid species, misidentification, hoaxes, or pareidolia — the human tendency to impose familiar patterns onto ambiguous stimuli.

In modern culture, Bigfoot has also become an icon. It appears in films, merchandise, roadside attractions, and tourism economies. This cultural saturation complicates perception rather than clarifying it.

This book does not approach Bigfoot as a zoological problem to be solved, nor as a symbolic fantasy to be dismissed. It approaches the phenomenon as a patterned interaction between human perception, ecology, and an adaptive intelligence that resists relational engagement.

— —

Pattern Reading

1. Bigfoot as a species
• Off-centre far right

• Small tree with branching only on the right

2. Bigfoot society
• Off-centre right
• Small, low, floating rectangle

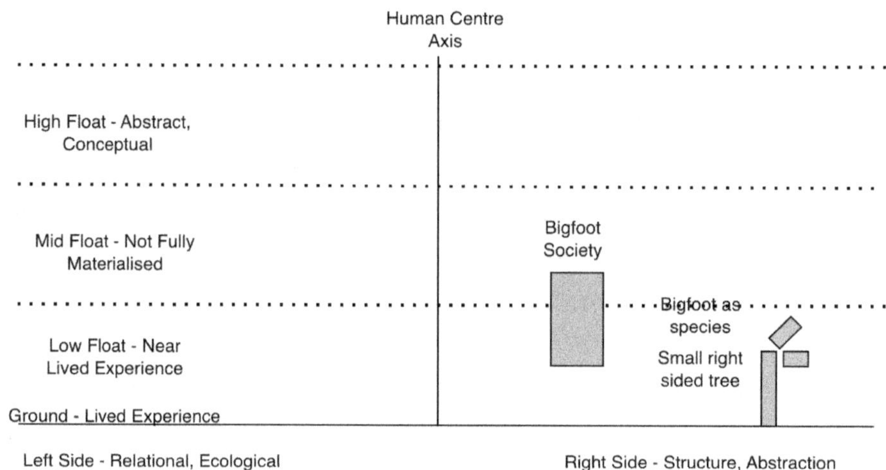

— —

Pattern Interpretation and Mapping

The species-level pattern shows a strongly right-side dominant intelligence. Right-side dominance emphasises prediction, avoidance, optimisation, and survival strategy. The absence of left-side branching indicates no relational orientation toward humans, no mythic self-expression, and no interest in shared meaning. The lack of centre branching suggests minimal reflection, mediation, or communicative impulse.

This is not a social or symbolic intelligence. It is an adaptive one.

The small size of the tree implies optimisation for persistence rather than expansion. This is not a species that builds culture, institutions, or cumulative knowledge systems. It does not externalise memory through tools, structures, or markings. Its intelligence is situational and immediate.

The far-right placement maps closely to reported Bigfoot behaviour: repeated evasion without pursuit, observation without engagement, proximity without escalation. Bigfoot does not initiate contact. It does not display dominance. It does not communicate. Humans are navigated around, not related to.

This places Bigfoot in an uncomfortable perceptual zone for modern humans. It appears too biological to be spiritual, too intelligent to be animal, too evasive to be studied, and too consistent to dismiss outright. As a result, perception collapses. The phenomenon oscillates between hoax, monster, joke, obsession, and belief. None of these frames hold for long.

From a perceptual lens, "Bigfoot" is the shape human perception gives to an intelligence occupying an ecological niche humans once inhabited but largely abandoned. The upright posture reflects shared locomotion and terrain. The human-like form indicates recognisable intelligence. Large size signals deterrence without aggression. Hair-covered embodiment reflects concealment, insulation, and non-technological survival. The absence of tools reflects an intelligence that never externalised cognition.

The second pattern — Bigfoot society — reinforces this. A small, low, floating rectangle off-centre right indicates minimal social structure, limited continuity, and non-grounded settlement. Floating suggests mobility and impermanence. Low placement reflects proximity to subsistence-level survival. The small scale suggests a sparse population.

If Bigfoot society exists at all, it likely consists of transient clustering rather than stable communities. Temporary association, dispersal, and withdrawal are favoured over continuity. This explains the absence of tools, dwellings, burial sites, or cumulative cultural residue.

Bigfoot does not function as a guardian, teacher, or messenger. Nor does it function as a mythic being in the traditional sense. It represents an adaptive intelligence that has successfully avoided integration with human systems. Its persistence is not evidence of mystery alone, but of a strategy that leaves no trace.

Mothman

Unlike Bigfoot, which is framed as a physical creature inhabiting remote wilderness, the Mothman is treated as a paranormal presence that appears in proximity to disaster.

The first recorded sightings occurred in 1966 in Point Pleasant, West Virginia. Witnesses described a seven-foot-tall humanoid figure with massive wings and glowing red eyes, first seen near an abandoned World War II munitions site. Over the following year, more than one hundred people reported encounters with the same figure, often accompanied by an overwhelming sense of dread.

The Mothman became permanently associated with the collapse of the Silver Bridge, which connected Point Pleasant to Ohio. When the bridge failed in 1967, killing forty-six people, the sightings were retroactively framed as either a warning of the disaster, or as causally linked to it.

A similar pattern appears decades later in accounts surrounding the Chernobyl nuclear disaster. Reports describe a large, dark, winged figure — sometimes called the "Black Bird of Chernobyl" — seen in the days leading up to the reactor failure.

Skeptical explanations suggest misidentification of large birds, such as owls, whose eyes reflect red under artificial light, combined with fear and poor visibility. While these explanations may account for individual sightings, they do not address the consistency of the pattern across time, location, and type of event.

— —

Pattern Reading

On the human centre axis:
- A long, hollow oval.
- Floating.

— —

Pattern Interpretation and Mapping

The long oval is a container without contents. It does not hold a message, an identity, or an intelligence. Modern perception attempts to collapse the Mothman into an entity — asking what it is, where it comes from, or what it wants — but these questions assume there is something inside the shape. There isn't.

The length of the oval indicates duration rather than immediacy. The phenomenon appears for a period of time before an event, not as a momentary signal. Its floating nature shows it is not ecological, embodied, or land-based. It does not belong to a terrain, species, or lineage.

Its placement on the human centre axis is critical. The Mothman intersects directly with human coherence — not belief, not mythic structure, but lived continuity. It appears where systems humans depend on are structurally fragile.

The hollow oval represents a cavity in coherence. A space where the present is no longer stable, but the future has not yet resolved. This creates a perceptual vacuum that manifests as unease, dread, and heightened attention without clarity. The Mothman does not announce what will happen. It exposes instability without offering resolution.

This is why encounters are experienced as disturbing rather than instructive. There is no guidance, no relational exchange, no symbolic teaching. Only exposure.

Unlike Bigfoot, which avoids human systems, the Mothman intersects them precisely at points of failure. Unlike totemic animals, which stabilise behaviour, the Mothman destabilises orientation without replacing it.

Human perception collapses this cavity into a figure. Glowing red eyes symbolise alertness without specificity — awareness without comprehension. The winged, shadowed form amplifies unease. Narrative then arrives to contain what cannot be held directly, transforming the phenomenon into folklore, prophecy, or entertainment.

In cultures with distributed orientation, such a phenomenon would not become a creature. It would be recognised as a boundary condition — a signal that a place, structure, or timing had become unsafe. The response would be withdrawal, not investigation.

The Mothman belongs to an industrial, infrastructure-dependent civilisation. It arises from scale, complexity, and cascading failure. It is not an ancient being resurfacing. It is a modern perceptual phenomenon produced by brittle systems under strain.

Past UFO Cases

Roswell

Possibly the most famous and most debated UFO event occurred in 1947 in Roswell, New Mexico. A rancher, William Brazel, discovered a strange debris field on his property, spread across an area roughly 180 metres in diameter.

(Author's note: In earlier decades, such sightings were referred to as Unidentified Flying Objects (UFOs), a term reflecting the assumptions of the time. In modern contexts, the term Unidentified Aerial Phenomena (UAP) is used, acknowledging that what is observed may not be an object at all. Terminology in this book will remain era-consistent.)

Brazel brought samples of the debris to the local sheriff, who, uncertain what he was looking at, contacted the military. The following day, a now-famous newspaper headline was published: "RAAF Captures Flying Saucer On Ranch In Roswell Region." Within hours, the story was retracted. The military revised its statement, explaining the debris as remnants of a weather balloon.

From that point onward, Roswell entered a state of suspension.

Debates have since revolved around whether the debris came from a weather balloon, a classified military project, or something non-human. In the decades that followed, later testimonies complicated the narrative further. During the 1970s and 1980s, researchers reported accounts attributed to Brazel's son and neighbouring witnesses, describing materials that could not be cut or burned, thin foil-like substances that returned to shape when crumpled, and fragments marked with unfamiliar, hieroglyphic-like symbols. None of these details appeared in Brazel's original 1947 interview.

Roswell became not a single event, but a long vertical accumulation of partial statements, revisions, silences, and contradictions.

From this book's perspective, the importance of Roswell lies less in what crashed, and more in how the event was processed. Roswell marks the first large-scale encounter between a fully right-side industrial civilisation and a phenomenon that does not resolve through right-side channels.

— —

Pattern Reading

Shapes sensed, describing distribution of meaning relative to the human centre:
- Off-centre right — tall plateau
- High far left — small, solid, floating circle
- Low far right — solid, floating pyramid

— —

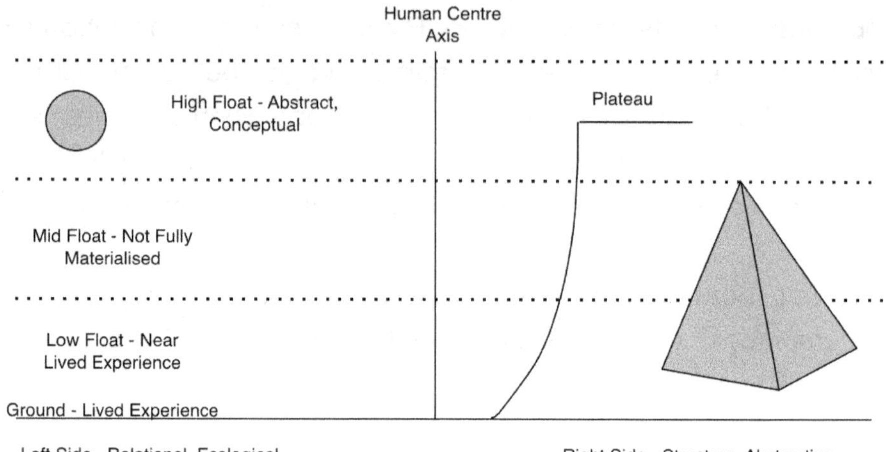

Pattern Interpretation and Mapping

The tall plateau on the right represents stabilised authority and established systems. Roswell occurred within a mature military-industrial context: centralised command, classified research, compartmentalisation, and a population accustomed to institutional explanations. The height of the plateau indicates confidence and operational dominance. This is a system designed to absorb anomalies and flatten them into acceptable narratives.

This maps directly to the Roswell response pattern: initial acknowledgement, rapid retraction, replacement explanation, and prolonged silence. The plateau maintains coherence by smoothing irregularities rather than resolving them.

The small, solid, floating circle represents a direct but limited encounter with left-side relational knowing. Its small size indicates low degree of condensation. Its solidity reflects certainty at the witnesses' personal level, while its floating quality shows the absence of embodiment or conceptual anchoring. Positioned far left, it exists outside the dominant interpretive structures of the time.

This maps to witness testimonies marked by clarity without closure: confidence without explanation, significance without language. The experience was real to those who encountered it, yet difficult to integrate into shared reality.

The solid, floating pyramid represents hierarchical containment. Low and floating, it operates operationally and out of public view. Positioned far right, it is distant from lived cultural perception. The pyramid's function is not interpretation but isolation—handling anomalies through secrecy, analysis, and restriction rather than open scientific inquiry.

Together, these shapes explain why Roswell remains unresolved. Direct perception cannot scale. Authority dominates narrative coherence. Hierarchy isolates information. The public is left with fragments—enough to sense distortion, but not enough to resolve it. Too much authority surrounds the event for it to be dismissed as trivial, and too little shared perception exists for certainty.

— —

The debris, or "materials"—whether fragments, artefacts, or bodies —are better understood as artefacts of forced interface. Right-side observation collapses and contains phenomena that do not naturally localise. Under sustained observation and containment, the field temporarily condenses into physical matter. These forms are unstable, inconsistent, and difficult to categorise.

This maps to the divergent descriptions of the materials. The inconsistencies are not evidence of deception alone, but of interface strain. Materials and stories alike are residues of interaction, not indicators of origin.

Why, then, did the "flying disc" become the primary container for meaning? When perception cannot complete itself, the mind stabilises experience into a coherent shape. The disc is a minimal, integrated geometry—balanced, bounded, and technologically neutral. It functioned as a temporary bridge between anomaly and civilisation.

Earlier left-side civilisations, with distributed orientation intact, would have recognised anomalies through shared relational knowing. Perception would precede explanation, and narrative containment may not have been required. By 1947, that capacity had largely eroded. Roswell represents the first large-scale right-side attempt to process an anomaly through authority, containment, and narrative control.

In doing so, it set the pattern for modern UFO and UAP culture—where encounters are filtered through symbols, expectations, secrecy, and fear, rather than integrated through lived coherence.

Rendlesham Forest

The Rendlesham Forest incident occurred in December 1980 near two NATO airbases — RAF Woodbridge and RAF Bentwaters — in Suffolk, England. It unfolded over multiple nights, through movement within a forest environment, and involved numerous military witnesses. There was no crash, no debris, and no single focal event.

It is sometimes referred to as "Britain's Roswell," but structurally, it is very different.

The first encounter occurred in the early morning hours of 26 December 1980. Security patrols reported strange lights descending into Rendlesham Forest. Personnel sent to investigate encountered a glowing object moving through the trees, described as metallic, with coloured lights. Animals on a nearby farm reportedly became agitated.

When the site was revisited in daylight, witnesses reported small triangular ground impressions, broken branches, and scorch-like marks. Radiation readings taken at the site were significantly higher than background levels in surrounding areas.

On the second night, 28 December, a further investigation was led by Lieutenant Colonel Charles Halt. Halt carried a micro-cassette recorder and captured approximately eighteen minutes of contemporaneous audio as the event unfolded. Witnesses again reported unusual lights, including a pulsating red light observed across a field. Skeptics later suggested this may have been Orford Ness Lighthouse, visible from the area.

The primary military witnesses have consistently stood by their accounts, emphasising that they were trained personnel familiar with aerial activity and environmental conditions, and that what they observed did not match known explanations.

— —

Pattern Reading

- Off-centre left
- A curve shaped like the left-side silhouette of a tree
- Floating

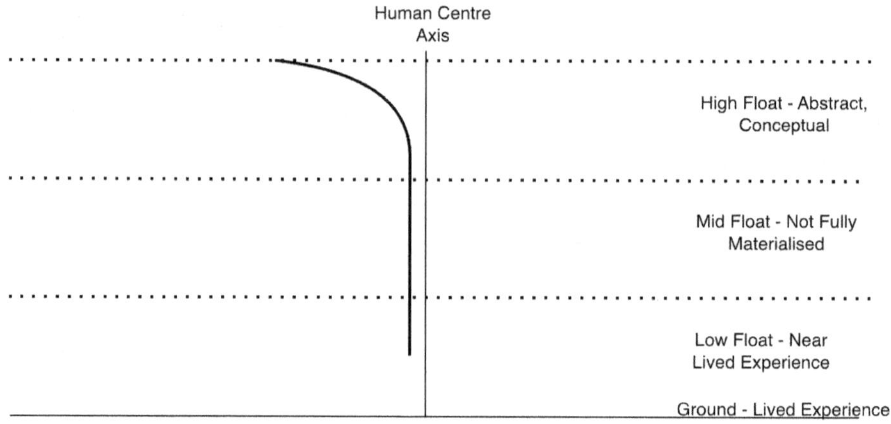

Conventional approaches ask what object appeared at Rendlesham, where it came from, and how it moved. From this lens, Rendlesham is not primarily about an object. It is about environment and relational behaviour.

— —

Pattern Interpretation and Mapping

The left-side curvature indicates an adaptive, non-directive, non-linear intelligence. The tree silhouette maps to a nature-based coherence: trunk as continuity, branches as multiple relational contact points, and presence distributed rather than localised. This is not transport behaviour. It is interface behaviour.

Roswell occurred within a dominant right-side civilisation encountering an external anomaly, resulting in immediate abstraction, containment, and narrative control. Rendlesham is the inverse. Here, humans entered an already coherent left-side field. The anomaly was not visiting the humans; the humans were moving into it.

Left-side phenomena do not announce themselves. They do not instruct or explain. They emerge through movement, attention, and proximity. This maps directly to the Rendlesham experience, which unfolded through walking, searching, stopping, and re-orienting. The phenomenon appeared responsive to attention rather than command.

Floating does not mean disconnected from land. It means the presence does not stabilise into a single reference point. The intelligence is distributed, mobile, and ambiguous. This corresponds with reports of shifting lights, unclear structure, unstable distance and size, and the absence of recoverable artefacts.

Forests naturally support distributed orientation. They are non-linear environments with layered sensory input, long continuity, and dense relational feedback. Such environments allow field-based intelligences to be present without collapsing into form. Animals, with intact field sensitivity, often register such shifts immediately, which aligns with the reported disturbance of nearby livestock.

When modern military perception — trained for threat identification and object classification — encountered this field-based phenomenon, the interface strained. The experience collapsed into lights, motion, proximity, intent, and anomalous readings such as radiation.

Rendlesham did not escalate. There was no isolatable object, no debris, no reproducible artefact. There was nothing for right-side systems to stabilise, test, or contain. The institutional response therefore became minimisation, ambiguity, and quiet archival dismissal. There was nothing actionable.

Rendlesham demonstrates that not all UFO encounters are visits by external entities. Some are encounters with environmental intelligences and field anomalies that modern perception no longer knows how to hold without forcing collapse.

Phoenix Lights

In March 1997, a widely witnessed, large-scale, multi-hour aerial phenomenon occurred over Arizona, United States. Witnesses described a nighttime event consisting of a series of lights arranged in the shape of a massive dark "V" or boomerang, moving slowly across the state. The formation was silent and large enough to obscure the stars as it passed overhead.

Later that same night, a separate set of lights appeared over the Estrella Mountains near Phoenix. These lights remained stationary for a period before disappearing one by one. This second event was the most widely recorded on video and became the dominant visual reference in media coverage.

The Phoenix Lights entered mass public awareness due to the sheer number of witnesses — numbering in the thousands — including police officers, pilots, and air traffic observers. Despite this, the event never resolved into certainty or dismissal.

The United States Air Force later explained the Estrella Mountain lights as illumination flares dropped during a training exercise. This explanation addressed part of the night's events, but not the earlier, city-wide passage of the large, silent formation. As a result, the incident remains structurally ambiguous.

——

Pattern Reading

Shapes sensed:
- Long left-curved line, originating at bottom centre, tilted approximately 10 degrees from vertical
- Off-centre mid-left: high, floating, solid small circle

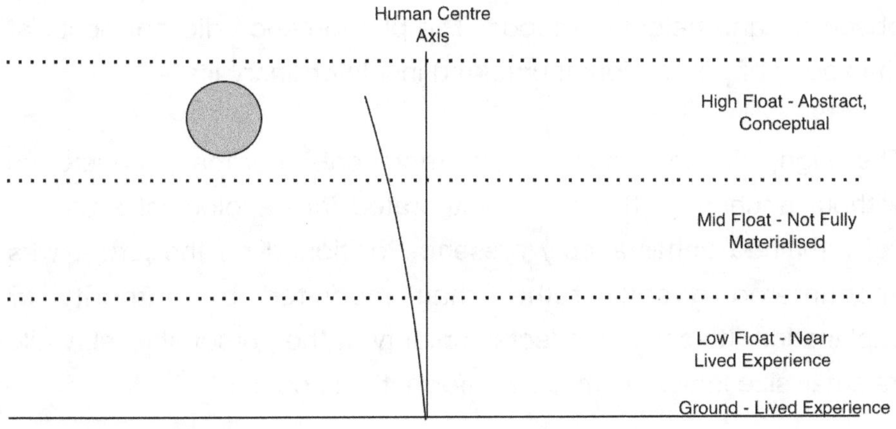

— —

Pattern Interpretation and Mapping

This configuration indicates a left-side distributed and relational presence rather than a discrete object.

The long curved line maps to duration and continuity. Curvature indicates adaptive, responsive movement rather than linear propulsion. Witness accounts frequently describe a sense of awe, stillness, and temporal dilation. As if the event unfolded with the environment, rather than through it.

Many witnesses reported sensing the phenomenon before seeing it, describing a heaviness, pressure, or displacement in the air. The left-side orientation corresponds to a relational or ecological field interaction — more akin to a silent wave or presence than a military or technological threat.

The origin at bottom centre places the event directly within lived human space. This maps to its wide visibility across independent observers and neighbourhoods. The phenomenon did not occur at the edges of perception; it unfolded inside ordinary life.

The high, floating, solid circle represents compact coherence without anchoring. It was not integrated into ecological systems, yet remained unmistakably present. Positioned on the left, it was encountered directly rather than mediated by authority or explanation. Its solidity reflects certainty at the personal level, while its small size indicates minimal informational content.

This explains a defining feature of the Phoenix Lights: the phenomenon scaled horizontally across observers without scaling in resolution. Thousands saw it. No one gained more clarity by observing it longer. The certainty did not deepen into explanation.

Without the circle, the incident could be dismissed as misperception. Without the curved line, it would collapse into a brief sighting. The circle is too solid to dismiss, too small to support narrative, and too floating to anchor intent or origin. It resists both belief and debunking.

The military explanation of illumination flares functions as narrative pressure release rather than resolution. It provides closure for part of the event without addressing its full structure.

Earlier left-side cultures may have marked such an occurrence as an omen, a seasonal threshold, or a recognised category of field behaviour. Modern culture, lacking shared relational sensing, no longer knows how to recognise without immediately narrating. The result is prolonged ambiguity rather than integration.

McMinnville Photos

The McMinnville UFO photos are two of the most famous and most debated photographs in the history of ufology. They were taken on a farm near McMinnville, Oregon, in May 1950. The images captured a disc-shaped object in the sky and went on to become one of the defining visual templates of the 1950s UFO era.

One evening in May 1950, Evelyn Trent was feeding farm animals when she noticed a metallic disc-shaped object moving across the sky. She called to her husband, Paul Trent, who retrieved his camera and managed to take two black-and-white photographs before the object disappeared.

The Trents did not immediately contact the press. They finished the roll of film over time and only later had it developed. A local banker reportedly displayed the prints in his window, where they caught the attention of a reporter from the McMinnville Telephone Register, which published them in June 1950. Within weeks, Life magazine featured the photographs, bringing national attention to the case.

Over the following decades, both the images and the Trents themselves were subjected to extensive scrutiny. The Trents were widely regarded as honest, grounded people with no history of seeking publicity. They never profited from the photographs and maintained their account consistently until their deaths in the late 1990s. Early analyses found the photographs broadly consistent with the stated conditions and testimony. Later sceptical explanations proposed that the object was a small model suspended by a thread from a power line.

Regardless of authenticity, the McMinnville photographs played a decisive role in shaping UFO culture. They helped stabilise the "metallic disc" as the default visual form of a UFO, embedding it deeply into public imagination and later reports.

— —

Pattern Reading, Interpretation, and Mapping

On centre axis: Grounded tall vertical line

A grounded vertical line on the centre axis is the signature of direct presence. It indicates something that appears plainly in human perception, without symbolic distortion or narrative amplification. This is not a mediated event, not a visionary encounter, and not something that collapses under observation. What is seen is simply what is there.

This is the pattern of an encounter-able physical reality.

The shape supports the interpretation that the photographs depict a discrete object rather than a perceptual artefact or symbolic projection. In that narrow sense, yes: it is a metallic flying disc.

What the shape does not specify is origin, intent, or meaning. It does not imply extraterrestrial source, higher intelligence, left-side relational contact, or communicative purpose. The pattern only confirms that the phenomenon presents itself as physically coherent within human sensory space.

This places the McMinnville case firmly in the category of unresolved physical phenomena. If anomalous events were to appear as ordinary objects rather than symbolic or mythic experiences, this is what they would look like.

— —

A second pattern reading was conducted on the intelligence associated with the McMinnville object.

Shape: Bottom-centre grounded. Straight vertical line with a slight rightward tilt (approximately 10 degrees).

The absence of curvature, enclosure, symmetry, or branching is significant. This is not a mythic intelligence, not a relational mediator, and not a symbolic carrier. It is an operational intelligence.

Bottom-centre grounding indicates full embodiment at the point of contact. Whatever intelligence is present operates directly in the physical domain. The shape does not suggest narrative continuity before or after the event; it only describes functionality during interaction.

The straight vertical line reflects directness and task-oriented function. There is no relational engagement, no signalling, no interpretive exchange. The intelligence does not adapt to human meaning-making. It performs, acts, or moves according to internal constraints rather than external perception.

The slight rightward tilt indicates minimal system orientation. This is not instinctual or biological intelligence, but neither is it abstract or symbolic. Structure is present, but only insofar as it enables operation. There is no excess complexity, hierarchy, or expression beyond what is required to function.

Operational intelligence, in this sense, refers to intelligence that manifests as execution rather than communication. It is defined by capability, not intention; by coherence of action, not relational awareness. It does not seek recognition, interpretation, or narrative placement.

——

Taken together, the object and intelligence patterns are internally coherent. The object is not a projection, and the intelligence does not require mythic scaffolding to stabilise it. The encounter does not provoke story, fear, reverence, or symbolic elaboration.

This is why the McMinnville photographs often feel flat to observers. There is little to interpret. No message, no escalation, no implied relationship. The images persist precisely because they resist meaning.

They show something present — and nothing more.

Men in Black

In UFO lore, the Men in Black are mysterious figures who appear shortly after a UFO sighting to intimidate witnesses into silence. They are consistently described as unsettling—not quite human, as if performing humanity rather than inhabiting it.

One of the earliest documented cases occurred in 1953. Albert Bender, director of the International Flying Saucer Bureau, abruptly shut down his successful UFO organisation. He later claimed he had been visited by three men dressed entirely in black, with glowing eyes, who warned him to stop his research. Bender reported that they communicated telepathically and that the encounter left him with severe headaches.

Across reports from the 1950s through the 1970s, Men in Black share a set of recurring traits that distinguish them from ordinary federal agents. They wear immaculate black suits with white shirts and black ties. Their skin is often described as pale or waxy. They speak in flat, monotone voices and use slang that is oddly outdated for the period. They frequently arrive in black Cadillacs or Buicks. Above all, witnesses report an overwhelming sense of unease or fear in their presence.

A well-known modern case occurred in Niagara Falls in 2008. Security footage from a hotel lobby captured two unusually tall, identical men wearing black trench coats and hats. Witnesses reported that they had no eyebrows or eyelashes, and piercing blue eyes that seemed to stare through people rather than at them. One staff member became physically ill during the encounter; another reported that the air in the room felt as though it had "changed." The men were allegedly seeking a manager who had recently reported a UFO sighting.

The most common explanation is that Men in Black are members of a covert government agency tasked with suppressing UFO information. Other theories propose that they are non-human entities or inter-dimensional beings attempting to mimic humans. Skeptics argue that Men in Black encounters are hallucinations or archetypal projections triggered by stress or trauma.

None of these explanations fully account for the consistency of the phenomenon.

— —

Pattern Reading

Shapes sensed, describing distribution of meaning relative to the human centre:

- On centre: a vertical hollow oval, touching the ground, open at the bottom, with a faint upward pulse.
- A wedge with its tip at ground centre, angled approximately 20 degrees to the right, its left edge touching the centre axis.

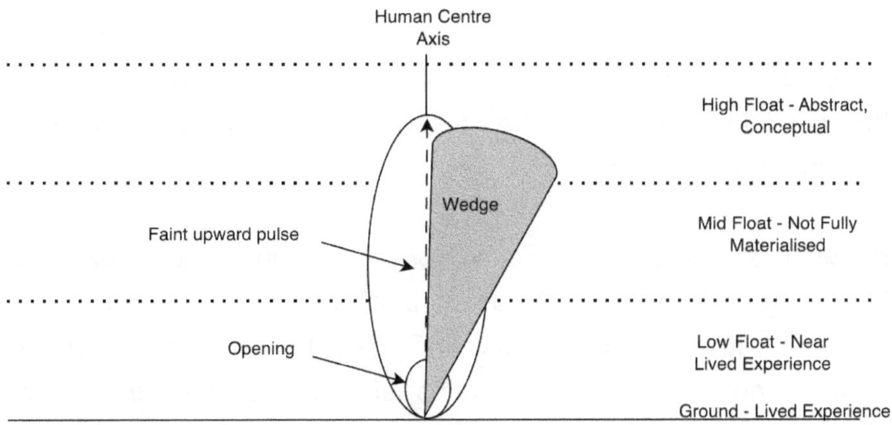

— —

Pattern Interpretation and Mapping

The vertical hollow oval is a human interface form, not an external being. Being hollow, it contains no intrinsic intelligence, personality, or agenda. It is a container without content. Touching the ground, it appears embodied and physically real—mapping directly to witnesses encountering them as "men."

The vertical orientation indicates that this form spans levels: bodily presence, authority, and meaning. It looks human and behaves procedurally human, but functionally acts as a channel rather than an agent. Its placement on the centre axis places it precisely at the human mediation layer—where raw perception is converted into meaning, and meaning into compliance.

The open bottom at ground level indicates that this form is fed by low-level emotional charge: fear, uncertainty, and destabilisation. The faint upward pulse suggests intermittent activation. Men in Black do not persist. They appear briefly, apply pressure, often exhibit signs of depletion or awkwardness, and then disappear. They activate specifically when ambiguity threatens to destabilise dominant narrative order.

The wedge represents narrative force—authority, reduction, and closure. Its directional pressure is applied at a single point: the individual witness, shortly after an encounter and before shared meaning can stabilise. The wedge's left edge touching the centre axis indicates interruption of human mediation. Sense-making is cut off before it can propagate socially.

Men in Black are not federal agents. They are not autonomous beings. They are a stabilisation reflex of the human meaning system. They are the shape authority takes when explanation is unavailable but compliance is still required.

This explains their consistent attributes:
• They are triggered into being.
• They are reactive and short-lived.
• They are hollow in content.
• They show strong structural consistency.
• They exist to prevent perception from becoming shared human reality.

This is why they appear after encounters, not before. They never provide new information. They discourage communication. They dissolve once their function is complete. This rules out intelligence agencies, non-human entities, and hallucinations as primary explanations.

Why, then, does human perception collapse this function into the specific form of Men in Black?

Because the phenomenon requires a minimal, efficient, and recognisable authority shape. Black suits signal hierarchy and control. Emotional flatness signals procedural authority. Identical appearance reduces individuality. The Men in Black are not chosen consciously; they are the most efficient shape available to terminate ambiguity.

They are not the mystery. They are the mechanism that stops the mystery from spreading.

Perceptual Interlude

Why Do Humans See the Same Shapes?

If anomalous phenomena like UFOs, cryptids and Men in Black are shaped by human perception — or at least partly co-created through observation — why do different people, separated by time, culture, and belief, so often report the same forms?

There are several possible explanations.

Hypothesis 1: Shared human perceptual limitations.
Humans share the same biology: visual systems, motion detectors, threat heuristics, and pattern-completion mechanisms. There are only so many ways an ambiguous stimulus can be resolved by this system.

Hypothesis 2: Cultural narrative gravity wells.
Cultures do not generate infinite myths. They generate forms that are easy to remember, transmit well, meet emotional needs, and do not destabilise social order. When ambiguity appears, people rarely invent freely; they default to available shapes.

Hypothesis 3: Constraint from the phenomenon itself.
Even if a phenomenon is not a craft or a creature, it may still operate under real constraints. Using plasma as a metaphor: plasma does not produce infinite appearances, but a family of related forms. Human perception is therefore guided, not free-form.

Hypothesis 4: Observation as a locking mechanism.

Observation does not create the phenomenon, but it stabilises one of its possible expressions. Early observers effectively "lock in" a form. Subsequent observers tune into that stabilised pattern, which persists because it is easier to perceive again — much like how a meme stabilises through repetition.

——

Three pattern readings offer insight into which of these explanations dominates.
• Pattern 1: Shape of Human Perception
• Pattern 2: Shape of Human Mediation
• Pattern 3: Shape of Human Perceptual Stabilisation

——

Pattern 1 – Shape of Human Perception

On centre: Short vertical grounded line

This represents a shared human perceptual baseline. Positioned on the centre axis, it exists prior to belief, culture, or narrative. The vertical line connects sensory input at the base, through cognition, to interpretation at the top.

Its short length is crucial. It is "just enough." Variation is limited. Imagination does not have unlimited freedom. As a result, outcomes cluster tightly. When ambiguity enters perception, humans do not generate infinite forms; they resolve into a small, repeatable set.

This constraint is grounded in physiology. It prevents excessive divergence. Once a perception passes through this bottleneck, it becomes describable, memorable, and transmissible.

— —

Pattern 2 – Shape of Human Mediation

On centre: Tall, steep, floating triangle

This shape describes the mediation layer — where raw experience acquires meaning, but before it becomes narrative. The triangle represents species-level compression.

A triangle implies pressure, selection, and reduction. A steep triangle means a wide range of sensory, emotional, and contextual input at the base, narrowing rapidly into an extremely limited range of conscious meaning at the apex. Ambiguity, delay, and complexity are actively selected against.

Floating indicates that this process is not consciously chosen. It evolved because rapid, repeatable interpretation kept humans alive. What ensured survival also traps perception into recurring archetypes.

— —

Pattern 3 – Shape of Human Perceptual Stabilisation

On centre: Small grounded square

This shape is not perception itself, but the stabilisation of perception. A small square is finite, bounded, repeatable, and conservative. It does not explore or interpret; it locks.

The square freezes interpretation so it can be relied upon and communicated. Without it, perception would remain fluid despite funneling. Myths would not stabilise. UFOs would not acquire standard forms. Symbols would drift endlessly.

The square is the minimum viable container for shared reality. Once an anomalous perception fits inside it, cultures adopt it, nervous systems reinforce it, and memory defends it.

Humans do not live inside perception. They live inside decisions made about perception.

Most red herrings in anomalous phenomena are not fabrications. They are early settlements produced by the modern human perceptual process.

— —

Taken together, these patterns align most closely with Hypothesis 1: shared human perceptual limitations. Humans encounter mystery not with open bandwidth, but through a survival-shaped funnel that produces and stabilises repeatable forms.

This model does not deny the existence of non-human intelligence or unknown crafts. It explains why humans so often mistake their own perceptual machinery for external agency — and, importantly, why the rare cases that do not fit this machinery deserve far more attention.

Past UFO Contacts

Ariel UFO Encounter

The 1994 Ariel School Encounter is one of the most significant close-encounter incidents in UFO history, involving reported contact rather than distant observation. The event is notable not only for its content, but for the number and consistency of witnesses: approximately sixty children at a private primary school in Ruwa, Zimbabwe.

The incident occurred mid-morning while the children were playing outside during recess. Several reported seeing one or more disc-shaped craft descend from the sky and land beyond the school grounds. At the time, the teachers were indoors attending a staff meeting.

One or two small beings were reported to have emerged from the craft. The children described them as approximately one to one-and-a-half metres tall, with pale faces, large dark eyes, and tight, dark clothing. Some witnesses described their movement as unusual or discontinuous — appearing briefly, blinking, or shifting position in ways that felt unnatural or "glitch-like."

Several children reported receiving impressions or messages through eye contact rather than speech. These impressions were described as warnings or concerns about environmental harm and humanity's relationship with the Earth.

Harvard psychiatrist Dr John Mack later travelled to Zimbabwe to interview the children individually and in groups. He concluded that the accounts did not resemble fabrication or mass hysteria, and that the children appeared to be describing a real, shared experience, even though they struggled to articulate it in conventional terms.

— —

Pattern Reading

Shapes sensed, describing distribution of meaning relative to the human centre:
- Near centre, off-centre left: grounded near-vertical line, curving slightly left (~15°)
- Far left: small, solid, floating triangle

— —

Pattern Interpretation and Mapping

The primary interaction shape sits on the left, but close to the human mediation axis. This places the encounter in the relational domain, while remaining accessible to human perception and memory. The grounded quality indicates that the experience was embodied and real to the witnesses, not dreamlike or dissociative.

The slight curve toward the left signals receptivity rather than imposition. There was no command, instruction, or authority asserted. Meaning arose through felt sense rather than explanation or narrative framing.

This maps to contact without hierarchy. The presence did not attempt to persuade, teach, or recruit. It appeared, was perceived, and left an imprint that remained coherent over time. This helps explain the consistency of the Ariel accounts: the children did not mythologise the experience. They described it plainly, relationally, and with emotional congruence — a consistency that persisted into adulthood.

The small floating triangle represents the message itself. A triangle indicates compression, selection, and efficiency. Its small size suggests limited scope. Its solidity indicates internal coherence. Positioned far left, it remains outside authority structures, belief systems, or doctrinal transmission. Floating indicates abstraction rather than instruction tied to action.

What was transmitted was not technology, prophecy, or ideology. It was a minimal relational signal — coherent, non-coercive, and non-directive. This maps directly to reports of non-verbal environmental concern, received as impression rather than language.

The reports of the beings appearing to blink or glitch in and out of perception are consistent with a field-level anomaly rather than a stable embodied entity. Human perception collapsed the interaction into familiar forms: UFOs, beings, and a message.

Why these forms? Likely because modern human culture is shaped by technological imagery and by a deep, often unspoken loneliness — the desire to believe we are not alone, and that more advanced intelligences might intervene or guide us away from self-destruction. In earlier eras, similar encounters may have been perceived as gods, spirits, or messengers.

— —

A separate pattern reading was performed for the shape of the intelligence behind the Ariel encounter:
Left side: medium-sized, grounded square

This indicates a relational and functional intelligence rather than an individuated being. A square represents boundedness, stability, repeatability, and conservative operation. Grounded placement ties this intelligence to land, ecology, and embodied systems.

Rather than an external visitor, this pattern is consistent with a regulatory ecological field intelligence — a stabilising function responding to imbalance. This maps cleanly to the content of the impressions received by the children, which centred on environmental concern rather than human hierarchy, technology, or destiny.

Barney & Betty Hill Encounter

In September 1961, Barney and Betty Hill were driving home to Portsmouth, New Hampshire, from a vacation. It was around midnight when they noticed a bright light in the sky that appeared to follow their car. Barney eventually stopped the vehicle and observed the light through binoculars. He described a large disc-shaped craft with lights, and figures visible through windows.

When they arrived home, they realised it was much later than expected. Approximately two hours of time could not be accounted for. In the days that followed, Betty began experiencing vivid, recurring nightmares involving being taken aboard a craft and subjected to examination.

In 1964, the Hills sought help from psychiatrist Dr. Benjamin Simon, who used regressive hypnosis as part of his therapeutic work. Under hypnosis, both Barney and Betty independently recounted detailed experiences of being taken aboard a craft by small humanoid figures and undergoing medical procedures.

One of the most widely cited elements of the case occurred during these sessions, when Betty drew a star map she said had been shown to her by the beings. Years later, the map was interpreted as corresponding to the Zeta Reticuli star system. This association later became foundational to the "Grey alien" narrative within UFO culture.

This case is generally regarded as the first widely publicised UFO abduction account in the United States.

— —

Pattern Reading
- A vertical line beginning at ground, touching both the centre axis and the left side, rising upward. Near the top, the line curves toward the right (~40° relative to vertical)
- A low, floating, solid pyramid on the right

— —

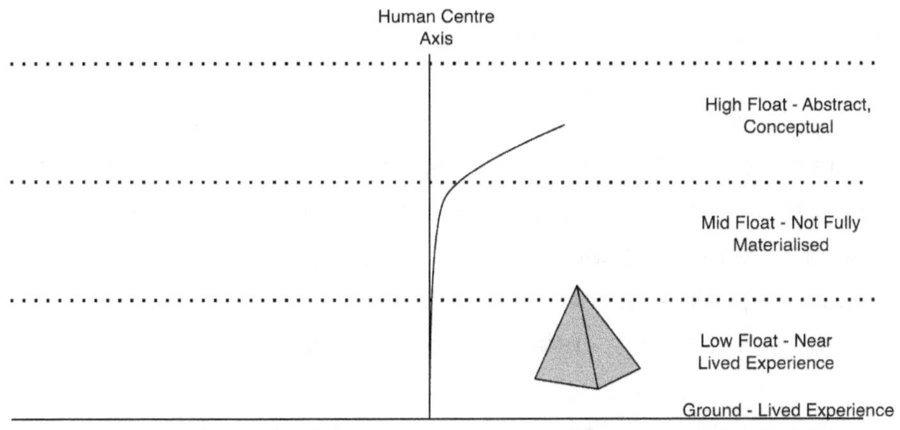

Pattern Interpretation and Mapping

The grounded vertical line touching the centre axis indicates direct perceptual engagement. This was not a purely abstract or symbolic experience; it was lived, embodied, and sensory. Its left-side contact reflects relational perception rather than authoritative interpretation. The experience entered awareness through direct encounter rather than pre-existing narrative.

As the line rises and curves toward the right, it reflects the later processing of the event through structured meaning-making. Hypnosis represents a human attempt to stabilise and integrate a left-side anomalous experience within a right-side dominant culture. Narrative, memory reconstruction, and symbolic framing appear only after the event, not during it.

This line-and-curve configuration illustrates a common pattern: left-side phenomena entering perception first, then being pulled toward right-side explanation in order to become communicable and survivable within modern consciousness.

The low, floating, solid pyramid on the right represents structured containment and procedural observation. Its low position indicates an operational, case-level function rather than institutional control. Its solidity reflects coherence and intention. This maps directly to the psychiatrist's role: not myth-making, but controlled extraction of memory and pattern under a formal methodology.

From this book's lens, the star map is not treated as navigational data or evidence of origin. It appears as a stabilising artefact. A geometric container generated during hypnotic reconstruction to hold an experience that could not otherwise be integrated. Maps reduce ambiguity by fixing location, distance, and meaning. Whether or not the configuration corresponds to an actual star system is secondary to its function: converting an unresolved perceptual rupture into a bounded, communicable narrative.

— —

A separate pattern reading was performed on the intelligence operating through the Barney and Betty Hill encounter:
- Right side
- High floating
- Small triangle

This configuration does not describe a relational or field-based intelligence. It is not embodied, ecological, emotional, or socially engaged. Its right-side placement indicates abstraction and system-level operation rather than relationship. This rules out many popular interpretations of benevolent or communicative extraterrestrial beings.

The triangle indicates reduction and selection — the narrowing of complex inputs into a small set of outputs. Its small size suggests a limited scope. This intelligence is not creative or adaptive; it performs a bounded function. High floating placement indicates detachment from embodiment and consequence. Empathy and consent are not part of its operational field.

This maps most closely to an interface logic rather than an agent in the human sense. Sampling, categorisation, calibration, and extraction are its primary modes. It does not relate to humans, but rather operates through them.

This explains the cold, procedural affect reported by the Hills. They did not feel met; they felt examined. The experience carries the tone of being processed rather than encountered. The intelligence was not "behind" the event in a narrative sense. Instead, its functional logic dominated the interface, shaping how the experience unfolded and how it was remembered.

Travis Walton Abduction

The Travis Walton abduction in November 1975 is unique in UFO lore because it involved multiple eyewitnesses who observed the initial event.

Walton was part of a seven-man logging crew working in the Apache–Sitgreaves National Forest near Heber, Arizona. One evening, while driving home in their truck, the crew saw a glowing, metallic, saucer-shaped craft hovering nearby. Walton exited the vehicle and approached the craft to get a closer look. As he neared it, he was struck by a beam of light and thrown backward. The other loggers, terrified, fled the scene in the truck. When they returned a short time later, both Walton and the craft were gone.

Law enforcement organised search parties, but no trace of Walton was found. He appeared to have vanished. Then, just after midnight, five days later, Walton's sister received a phone call from him. He was calling from a phone booth in Heber, sounding confused and disoriented, and insisting that only a few hours had passed.

Under hypnosis and in later debriefs, Walton described an experience dominated by fear. He reported that after losing consciousness, he awoke on a table inside a craft, surrounded by three short, hairless beings with large eyes. He fought them off before they left the room. He then moved through the craft and eventually reached what he believed was a control room containing a single chair and a viewing screen. Later, he encountered human-looking beings, after which he was put to sleep again. When he awoke, he found himself back in Heber.

No meaningful communication took place between Walton and the beings. In later years, Walton softened his interpretation of the event, suggesting that the beings may have taken him aboard to repair injuries caused by the accidental energy discharge from their craft.

The Walton abduction remains heavily debated due to conflicting evidence. Five of the loggers passed polygraph tests, with one result initially inconclusive and later passed. Walton himself has taken multiple polygraph tests over the years, with mixed results.

——

Pattern Reading

- A vertical line beginning at ground, touching both the centre axis and the left side, rising upward. Near the top, the line curves toward the left (~40° relative to vertical). (This is a mirror shape of the Barney and Betty Hill encounter)
- A low, floating, solid pyramid on the right

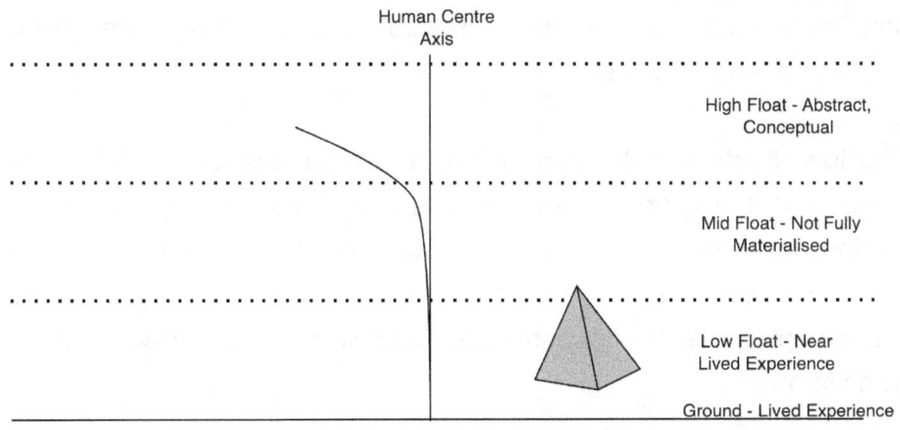

——

Pattern Interpretation and Mapping

The grounded vertical line indicates that the encounter was directly experienced by Walton. This was a physical, embodied event.

Touching both the centre axis and the left shows that the encounter occurred within the human stratum while remaining relational and ecological in nature.

As the experience progressed, the line curves further toward the left, indicating increasing relational intensity without corresponding right-side narrative integration. Unlike the Hills' encounter, there was no stabilising movement toward abstraction or meaning-making. Without adequate right-side processing, the experience overwhelmed human perception. The result was fragmentation, fear, and loss of agency.

This maps directly to Walton's inconsistent test results and to the way his recollection of the event shifted over time. Without narrative stabilisation, memory did not consolidate. Instead, it remained fluid, pressured, and reactive.

The low, floating, solid pyramid on the right represents right-side containment responses: law enforcement involvement, polygraph testing, investigations, and media framing. These actions handled the event operationally but did not generate meaning or help Walton integrate the experience. Containment occurred without translation.

——

A separate pattern reading was performed on the intelligence operating through the encounter:
• Right side
• High floating
• Six-pointed star

This configuration describes a system-oriented intelligence that is non-relational and detached from human experience. The six-pointed star indicates multiple simultaneous vectors — intersecting functions rather than a single coherent interface. There is no unified mode of engagement.

Its effect on Walton was overload. Unlike the Hills' encounter, where the interface logic was triangular and reductive, this configuration was dynamic and entangling. It neither acted toward Walton nor with him, but pulled him into overlapping processes without stability.

This maps closely to the nature of Walton's experience. The encounter lacked coherence, consent, and structure. It was not experienced as observation or communication, but as interference. Human perception was overwhelmed rather than guided.

The terror of the encounter did not arise from malice on the part of the intelligence, but from incompatibility between human perception and the interface logic at play.

Recent UAP Cases

Tic Tac Incident

The Tic Tac incident is widely considered one of the most credible UAP encounters in modern history. This 2004 event was corroborated by radar data, advanced cockpit sensors, and eyewitness testimony from U.S. Navy pilots.

The incident took place in November 2004 off the coast of Southern California during a Navy training exercise involving the USS Nimitz carrier strike group. Two pilots were diverted from the exercise to investigate an anomalous radar contact.

When the pilots reached the location, they observed a disturbance in the ocean below. Hovering above it was a smooth, white, oblong object roughly 12 metres long. No visible propulsion systems were present. The object—later referred to as the "Tic Tac"—began to mirror the movements of one of the aircraft, then accelerated suddenly at a speed far beyond known human aviation capability and vanished.

Moments later, radar operators informed the pilots that the object had reappeared nearly 100 kilometres away at the pilots' classified rendezvous coordinates. As if it knew.

A second pilot later launched with an infrared targeting system and managed to lock onto the object. This footage—now known as the Nimitz video—was leaked in 2007 and officially declassified by the Pentagon in 2020.

The Tic Tac exhibited characteristics now commonly associated with UAPs: apparent anti-gravity lift, instantaneous acceleration, hypersonic velocity, low observability, and trans-medium movement —the ability to move seamlessly between air and water.

This incident became a landmark moment in the modern UAP disclosure movement. It involved credible military witnesses, confirmation of a Pentagon program investigating similar encounters, and a demonstrated performance gap far beyond contemporary human technology.

——

Pattern Reading

Off-centre right: floating curve, resembling the top-left quarter of a circle.

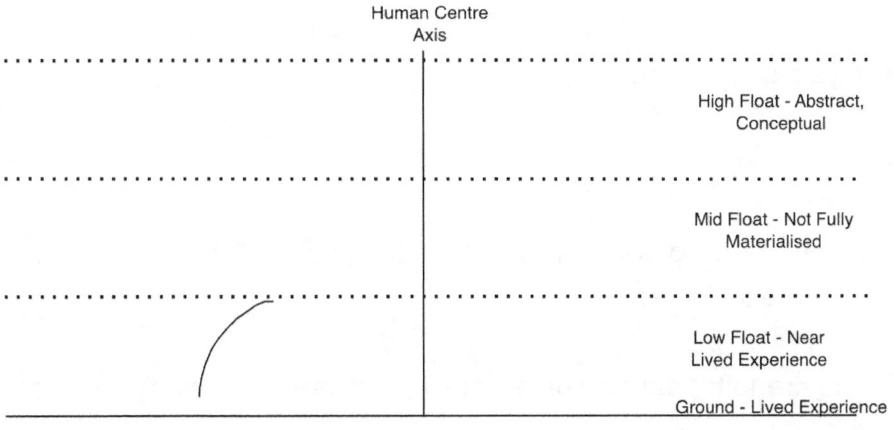

Pattern Interpretation and Mapping

The phenomenon entered human awareness from the right side. It was detected and tracked using technological systems—radar, infrared sensors, aircraft, and command infrastructure. The human response was procedural, hierarchical, and systems-based.

The shape is floating, indicating that the phenomenon was not embedded in land, ecology, or culture. It did not belong to the human world. The top-left quarter-circle curve places it high in the right-side domain—at a strategic or conceptual altitude. The left-facing curvature suggests relational information was present, but only partially accessible. Being only a quarter, humans perceived a slice of a much larger pattern.

The Tic Tac appears here as an anomaly brushing against right-side systems: coherent enough to be registered, but not enough to stabilise into a narrative. This helps explain why pilots described it as reactive, unreadable, non-hostile, non-communicative, and always a step ahead.

A second reading was performed on the shape of the "intelligence" behind the incident:

Off-centre left: floating curve, top-right quarter of a circle (a mirror of the first).

The origin of the coordination is relational and field-based, not hierarchical or command-driven. It is not incarnate, indicated by its floating quality. The mirrored arc suggests it belongs to the same pattern family as the right-side detection, but approached from the opposite side.

Being the right-facing arc of the left-side curve means it can interface with systems and respond to right-side activity without being part of those systems.

Whatever coordinated the incident does not resemble intelligence as humans understand it. It is not intentional in a communicative sense. It does not plan, instruct, or reveal. It is a field-level function capable of registering right-side systems and responding to them without dialogue, embodiment, or motive.

The mirroring is key:
• Humans detected a right-side quarter of the pattern
• The source occupied the left-side quarter
• The curvature and altitude match

Both were touching the same system from opposite sides.

Humans interpreted the encounter as evidence of superior intelligence because when right-side systems meet a response they cannot dominate or predict, they default to assuming hierarchy. This was not an encounter with advanced technology. That appearance arose through perceptual collapse. What occurred was a boundary interaction: one system registering another. No message. No intent. No exchange.

——

A third reading was performed on the system both shapes were interacting with:

Small, solid, floating circle on the left

This is neither the UAP nor its coordinator. It is the shared substrate both sides were touching.

The shape indicates a relational, field-based, non-authoritative system. Its small size suggests limited scope. Its solidity indicates stability and repeatability. Being floating, it does not reside in the physical human world. As a circle, it is self-contained and complete.

This immediately rules out several interpretations. Based on the shape, the system is:
- Not an alien civilisation (too small, no hierarchy)
- Not a consciousness observing humanity (no centre or intent vector)
- Not a craft origin point (no embodiment)
- Not a "higher intelligence" (no asymmetry or dominance)

What it could be is a natural response mechanism of reality itself—activated when certain conditions stack simultaneously: high-energy concentrations around carrier groups, dense technological sensor arrays in operation, tightly coordinated systems, and sustained focused attention.

Under those conditions, a pressure point appears. The resulting boundary effect registers differently on each side. On the human side, it collapses into an object. On the field side, it remains non-local and non-agentic.

——

There is something real occurring here—without any intelligence orchestrating it, without guidance offered, without threat implied, and without a narrative that satisfies human expectation.

We are not being watched.

Humans, through increasingly dense technological coherence, are pressing into a seam in reality.

Gimbal Incident

The Gimbal incident took place in January 2015, off the coast of Florida. It is significant because it features a video recording of a UAP displaying an apparent physical rotation in mid-air.

The incident involved pilots from the USS Theodore Roosevelt carrier strike group. The encounter was primarily captured via the Advanced Targeting Forward-Looking Infrared (ATFLIR) pod on a fighter jet.

The pilots reported seeing a fleet of around half a dozen smaller objects flying in a loose wedge formation ahead of the main "Gimbal" object. The primary object appeared as a spinning-top or saucer-like shape, surrounded by a glowing halo. As the pilots tracked it, the object performed a sudden, smooth tilt or rotation while maintaining its flight path against high-velocity winds. This apparent rotation is what led to the "Gimbal" name.

Despite travelling at high speeds, the object showed no heat plume or exhaust typical of jet propulsion. Under infrared, it appeared darker than the surrounding sky, indicating it was cold. Yet it was surrounded by a luminous halo that researchers have suggested may represent a field effect or some form of distortion rather than emitted heat.

Skeptics argue that the rotation seen in the video is not the object itself, but the internal gimbal mechanism of the infrared camera rotating to maintain lock on the target. From this perspective, the saucer-like appearance is attributed to infrared glare from a distant jet engine exhaust, shaped by the optics of the sensor system.

The pilots counter that radar data showed a solid object with distinct flight characteristics, consistent across multiple sensor systems and matching what they observed directly, independent of any camera artefact.

— —

Pattern Reading

Shape: Long, slightly curved line rising to the left (~10°), originating from mid-centre ground.

— —

Pattern Interpretation and Mapping

The line originates from the centre ground, indicating that the phenomenon appeared within active human operational space. This was not a distant or abstract anomaly; it emerged while human systems were already engaged. The length of the line indicates sustained presence and tracking over time, rather than a brief or transient event.

The gentle upward curve toward the left suggests increasing relational engagement rather than escalation through force. The Gimbal did not challenge human systems, evade detection, or provoke confrontation. It remained present, stable, and detectable. The curve implies adaptive response—adjusting to surrounding conditions rather than asserting dominance.

This maps closely to the pilots' experience. The Gimbal could be tracked, followed, and observed. It stayed just inside the threshold of engagement: visible and coherent, but without initiating interaction or communication. The incident was one of co-presence rather than encounter.

— —

A further reading was performed on the shape of the "intelligence" associated with the incident.

Shape: Left side. Small, solid, floating square.

This does not indicate intelligence as humans typically define it. Left-side placement suggests a relational, non-hierarchical function rather than command or intent. Its small size indicates limited local scope. Being solid, it is stable and repeatable. Floating indicates that it is not embodied or anchored to physical infrastructure.

The square represents stabilisation. This is a mechanism that holds a condition in place. This maps to the consistent behaviour observed during the Gimbal incident: no escalation, no engagement, and a narrow, repeatable behavioural band.

The Gimbal UAP is therefore unlikely to represent a craft outperforming human technology, or an intelligence testing military response. Instead, it appears consistent with a field-level stabilisation response.

Like the Tic Tac incident, this may reflect a natural boundary response of reality itself—activated under conditions of high-energy concentration, dense sensor arrays, tightly coordinated technological systems, and sustained focused attention. Under these conditions, a pressure point forms. The resulting stabilisation response is then perceptually collapsed by humans into the appearance of a craft. The fact that the object registered as cold under infrared is consistent with a field level response rather than a heat generating propulsion system.

Why UFOs Cluster Around Nuclear Sites

One of the most persistent patterns in UFO and UAP reports is their proximity to nuclear infrastructure. Sightings cluster around missile silos, weapons testing ranges, nuclear power plants, enrichment facilities, and storage sites. This pattern has fuelled a comforting narrative: that non-human intelligences are monitoring us, protecting us from ourselves, or intervening to prevent planetary catastrophe.

This interpretation appeals deeply to human psychology. It preserves the idea that we are not alone. It reassures us that someone more advanced is watching. It implies that technological superiority comes with moral oversight, and that if things become truly dangerous, someone will step in. It outsources our responsibility for ourselves.

This is not what the structural pattern suggests. The clustering is real. The meaning commonly assigned to it is not.

— —

Pattern Reading

Off-centre left: Low floating. Exponential curve. Ramp increasing toward the left

This is not a surveillance shape. It is not a defensive posture. It is not an intervention arc. This is a sensitivity curve.

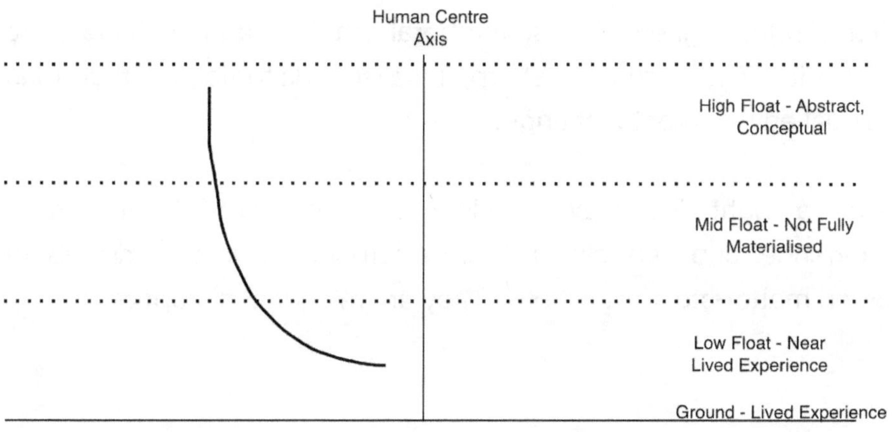

— —

Pattern Interpretation and Mapping

Left-side placement indicates a relational, non-authoritative process. Whatever is occurring is not issuing commands, warnings, or judgements. It is responding, not directing.

Low floating means the interaction is not fully embodied, but it is also not abstract or distant. It operates close to material reality without being fully anchored in it.

The exponential curve is the key. An exponential curve does not scale linearly. It remains quiet until a threshold is crossed, and then response increases rapidly. The ramp rising toward the left indicates that the response strengthens as relational disruption increases, not as technological sophistication increases.

This maps cleanly to nuclear activity. Nuclear sites are not merely technological landmarks. They are coherence disruptions. They alter electromagnetic fields, temporal stability, and material-state continuity. They produce sharp, localised distortions rather than gradual environmental change.

From a right-side view, nuclear weapons are about power, deterrence, and geopolitics. From a left-side view, they are about forced matter-state transitions. They are relational disruptions.

— —

Nuclear reactions do something unusual. They collapse vast amounts of potential into immediate, irreversible state change. They bypass many of the gradual buffering layers through which matter, energy, and systems usually adapt.

This creates environments that are highly constrained, energetically extreme, and difficult to integrate relationally. If anomalous phenomena operate through field sensitivity, phase instability, or boundary layer interactions, nuclear sites become natural hot spots. Not because those hot spots are being watched, but because they light up as stress fractures in the field.

— —

UFOs do not cluster around nuclear sites because humans are in danger. They cluster because nuclear activity produces conditions that stresses the field. This is why sightings spike near tests, crises, escalations, and transitions. Not steady-state operations.

The exponential curve explains this precisely. Below a certain threshold, nothing appears. Once crossed, visibility rises sharply. This creates the illusion of intention.

— —

Humans do not want to believe we are alone in our responsibility. The idea that advanced beings might intervene allows us to externalise accountability and preserve hope without behavioural change. The belief that "they have better technology and can help us" is a displacement strategy. It replaces the burden of responsibility with the fantasy of rescue. But the pattern offers no evidence of rescue behaviour. Only presence near thresholds.

The sobering reality is UFOs around nuclear sites do not imply guardianship. They imply proximity to instability. They indicate that whatever these phenomena are, they become more visible where coherence is stressed, boundaries are thinned, and matter is forced into unnatural transitions. This does not mean nuclear weapons threaten "them." It means nuclear activity distorts the conditions under which we normally experience reality. And in those distortions, things appear through our perception. A field under stress does not respond randomly. It expresses symmetry, minimal geometry, stable forms, energy efficient configurations. Discs, spheres, and ovals are field-efficient shapes.

Humans keep mistaking this for intelligence because humans are not used to non-agent regulation. We assume if it moves, it chooses. If it responds, it intends. Evolution trained humans to detect predators and allies, not fields.

Why UAP Disclosure Keeps Failing

For over seventy years, there has been a recurring expectation that "disclosure" is imminent. Each decade brings renewed anticipation: leaked documents, whistleblowers, declassified footage, congressional hearings, official task forces. And yet, despite increasing acknowledgment that anomalous aerial phenomena exist, the sense of resolution never arrives.

Disclosure is always described as being just ahead. And yet, it never seems to eventuate.

This persistent failure is usually attributed to secrecy, corruption, or deliberate suppression of truth. Governments are accused of hiding alien technology. Military institutions are assumed to possess answers they refuse to release. The public narrative frames disclosure as a withheld object — information that exists fully formed somewhere, waiting to be revealed.

But this framing assumes something crucial. It assumes that disclosure is a delivery problem. And that assumption may be wrong.

If disclosure were simply about releasing data, it should have succeeded by now. Sensor recordings, pilot testimonies, declassified reports, and official admissions already exist in the public domain. The United States government has acknowledged that some observed phenomena remain unidentified, demonstrate unusual flight characteristics, and are not attributable to known foreign technology.

And yet, rather than resolving the issue, each disclosure event seems to generate more confusion, more speculation, and more fragmentation.

The problem is not a lack of information. The problem is that information does not integrate. Right-side evidence does not transmit left-side experience. UAPs resist repeatability and fixed models. Modern human perception collapses the phenomenon into fragments. (Also see note below.)

As relational coherence collapses, interpretation rushes in to fill the gap. Fragments are pulled into belief or dismissal, polarising understanding. "Alien bodies" and unstable materials appear as temporary forms imposed by observation, not as stable entities within the phenomenon's own framework. Even if governments have these "physical evidence", they are likely unstable and hollow partial shells.

This suggests that disclosure is not failing because the truth is hidden, but because the "truth" being released is not stable.

Modern disclosure efforts attempt to resolve anomalous phenomena using the same frameworks that produced the opacity in the first place: hierarchical authority, technical abstraction, and narrative containment. These are right-side systems designed to manage risk, preserve coherence, and prevent destabilisation — not to integrate ambiguity into shared reality.

Disclosure assumes that once an authoritative institution confirms something, meaning will follow. Authority can release statements, footage, and reports, but it cannot generate shared relational perception. It cannot create lived coherence. It can only assert.

There is also a less discussed factor. Humans want disclosure to resolve into reassurance.

We want confirmation that we are not alone. That someone more advanced is watching. That there is intelligence beyond our own capable of guiding, correcting, or rescuing us. When disclosure does not deliver this meaning — as has consistently been the case — it is rejected, deferred, or endlessly reinterpreted.

Based on the cases examined in earlier chapters, this disclosure pathway appears fundamentally unlikely.

Disclosure keeps failing because it is being asked to do something it cannot do: translate an unresolved field phenomenon into a completed narrative without changing the perceptual framework of the civilisation receiving it.

What we are seeing instead is partial disclosure. Pressure release rather than integration. Data without coherence. Acknowledgement without shared perception.

UAPs are not visitors arriving to be revealed. They are exposures. They reveal the limits of human perception itself. Disclosure has failed and continue to fail, not because the truth is hidden, but because the civilisation attempting to receive it is not structured to carry it relationally.

— —

(Note: Anomalous phenomena do not require human observers to appear as objects. They require sufficient constraint. Cameras and sensors provide that constraint, not by intention, but by demand for legibility.

Instruments collapse fields into forms just as perception does, but into different geometries. Humans are centre-based mediators. Machines are right-side mediators. They collapse different aspects of the same anomaly into measurable parameters. What gets recorded are partial traces. Enough to disturb certainty, but not enough to stabilise meaning.)

— —

The failure of disclosure is not confined to the sky.

The same perceptual limits that prevent integration of UAP phenomena also appear when anomalous interaction occurs at ground level — particularly in environments where human orientation is already marginal. Dense wilderness, transitional terrain, and regions with limited relational landmarks amplify this effect.

This is where Missing 411 belongs.

These cases are often framed as mysteries of crime, predation, or hidden intelligence. But when examined through the same lens applied to UAPs, a different pattern emerges.

Missing 411 does not represent a new phenomenon. It represents the same field interaction — expressed where the human body, rather than technology, is the primary interface.

Strange Places

Missing 411

The Missing 411 phenomenon encompasses thousands of cases of people disappearing in seemingly ordinary national parks, forests, and wilderness areas in North America.

Across decades, the cases share a set of recurring characteristics:
- Individuals vanish quickly, sometimes with someone else nearby and minimal loss of line of sight.
- Certain demographics appear disproportionately represented: children, the elderly, neurodivergent individuals, solitary people, and experienced outdoors people.
- Footprints and tracks terminate abruptly, with no trace beyond a certain point.
- Personal belongings, clothing, and gear are sometimes left behind—occasionally arranged in ways that appear deliberate.
- Unusual environmental conditions are reported, including sudden fog, heavy rain, and animals behaving out of character.
- Search efforts frequently fail to locate the missing person, even under optimal conditions.

——

Pattern Reading

The dominant shapes sensed for this phenomenon are:
- The wedge — point at the bottom centre axis, one side flush with centre, the other angled approximately 30° to the left

- Off-centre left: a medium, hollow, grounded pyramid

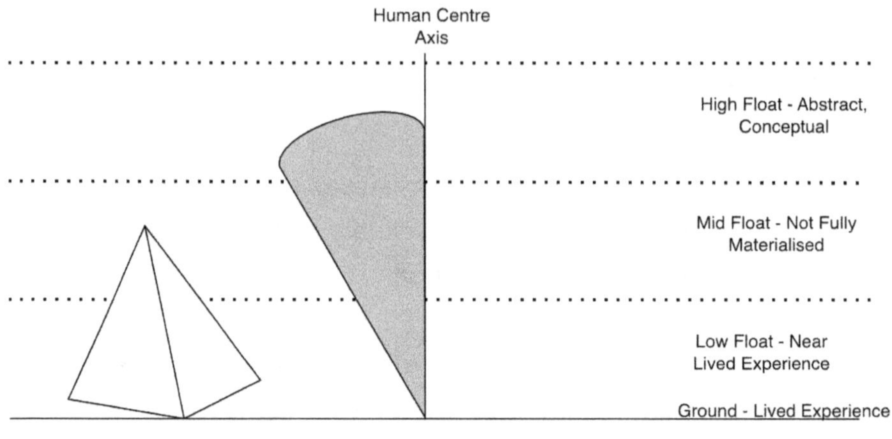

——

Pattern Interpretation and Mapping

The wedge is a transition geometry. It does not indicate intelligence or intent. The point at the bottom centre represents a precise moment of contact at the human baseline—where life is embodied and activity is ordinary. These cases occur during normal human movement: walking, hunting, foraging, playing, travelling through familiar terrain.

One side of the wedge sits flush with the centre. The phenomenon overlaps seamlessly with human reality. There is no escalation, no warning, no perceptual rupture. The transition is subtle enough that the individual may not register it at all.

The other side of the wedge angles left, indicating relational field divergence. The person does not move in a physical direction such as up, down, left, or right. Instead, they slip sideways relative to human coherence—into a different phase of the same space they are already occupying.

This maps directly to the core features of Missing 411 cases: no signs of struggle, footprints ending suddenly, scent trails stopping abruptly, and search dogs losing track without explanation.

The hollow pyramid on the left explains why these disappearances feel intentional without being driven by intent. Left-side placement rules out predatory behaviour, planning, or intelligence. What is operating here is ecological and field-based. Because the pyramid is grounded, the phenomenon occurs in Earth terrain—forests, mountains, wilderness zones.

Its hollowness is critical. This is a containment geometry. Once a person slips phase, they are held within a stable exclusion zone. They are no longer accessible to normal human tracking, time, or narrative continuity.

This explains why some individuals are later found alive but disoriented, sometimes far from their original location, sometimes in areas already searched, and often with reports of time distortion. The pyramid stabilises the disappearance itself, allowing it to persist without resolution.

——

What is occurring in Missing 411 is not abduction, predatory hunting, or inter-dimensional travel. It is closer to a local coherence failure—a boundary condition that humans cannot perceive until it is crossed.

Humans navigate terrain with an implicit assumption of perceptual continuity. In this phenomenon, that assumption fails. The wedge marks the point where human continuity and environmental continuity decouple. Once decoupled, motion is no longer proportional to distance, location is no longer stable, and time no longer accumulates linearly.

This maps cleanly to the reported characteristics:
- Footprints ending abruptly: the human body ceases to exert force into the same observable layer once phase coherence shifts.
- Clothing and personal items left behind: loose layers of human orientation do not phase along with the person. These remain as residues of the decoupling process, often appearing as if the person vanished in place. This also maps to cases where bodies are found unclothed or partially clothed.
- Environmental anomalies: sudden fog, silence, or altered animal behaviour are side effects of the ecological field adjusting to the discontinuity.
- Failure of searches: standard search methods operate entirely within the human perceptual layer. Once a person phases, those methods no longer apply.
- Reappearance or permanent absence: the individual may reappear in the original location, elsewhere, or remain outside human perception indefinitely.

——

Certain demographics appear more frequently in these cases, not due to weakness, but exposure.

Children have incomplete perceptual stabilisation. Their sense of continuity and boundary is still forming. They move more fluidly between attention states, embodiment, and time perception, making them lighter in their attachment to a single phase. This also explains why children are more often found alive—they reintegrate more easily.

The elderly are often in a stage of life where bodily anchoring is loosening. Metabolic rates slow, future-oriented cognition decreases, and narrative pressure thins. They are less rigidly locked into a phase.

Neurodivergent individuals frequently have atypical sensory processing. Centre-axis stabilisation is reduced, and perception is less tightly bound to consensus reality. This increases vulnerability to boundary effects.

Solitary individuals lack perceptual reinforcement. Groups stabilise coherence through shared attention. Disappearances often occur when someone steps away briefly, moves ahead, or lags behind—precisely where coherence thins.

Experienced outdoors people are affected more often than expected. Experience does not protect against phase transitions. In some cases, it increases exposure. Skilled outdoors people move quietly, follow animal paths, operate at liminal times such as dawn and dusk, and are comfortable in silence. These are edge states where field transitions are more likely.

None of this implies frailty. It implies proximity.

— —

Missing 411 is a reminder that humans do not fully inhabit the relational layers of the land. This is a subtle, field-based phenomenon—neither conscious, nor intelligent, nor cruel, but real and consequential.

The most unsettling aspect is not that something is acting, but that the world itself does not always behave as a single, continuous surface.

Skinwalker Ranch

Skinwalker Ranch is a 500+ acre property in northeastern Utah that is widely considered one of the most intensively studied anomalous sites in the world. For decades, it has been the location of a wide range of unexplained incidents, including reported UFO sightings, cattle mutilations, and encounters with strange creatures and beings.

According to local Ute tradition, the ranch lies in the path of the "Skinwalker," a malevolent shapeshifter. The Ute avoided the land for generations as a result.

In modern history, the ranch passed through three distinct phases of ownership:

Terry and Gwen Sherman (1994–1996)
The Shermans purchased the ranch to raise cattle. Within two years, they reported repeated cattle mutilations, encounters with

abnormally large wolves that appeared unaffected by gunshots, blue orbs, and what were described as portal-like phenomena.

Robert Bigelow (1996–2016)
The billionaire acquired the ranch to conduct a formal, long-term scientific investigation. Scientists lived on-site around the clock, deploying cameras, sensors, and monitoring equipment. Many documented events appeared to occur just outside sensor range or at moments of equipment failure, suggesting a reactive or responsive environment rather than random anomalies.

Brandon Fugal (2016–present)
The current owner has allowed research to be documented publicly through the History Channel series The Secret of Skinwalker Ranch.

Visitors and researchers frequently report sudden, unexplained illnesses, including microwave-like burns, nausea, headaches, and neurological symptoms. Some also report that anomalous experiences appear to persist after leaving the ranch.

Because the reported phenomena span so many categories, explanations range from the scientific to the supernatural. None have adequately accounted for the full pattern.

——

Pattern Reading

- A concave bowl at ground level, spanning left–centre–right
- Three vertical, tornado-like columns within the bowl (left, centre, right)

This is an environmental structure.

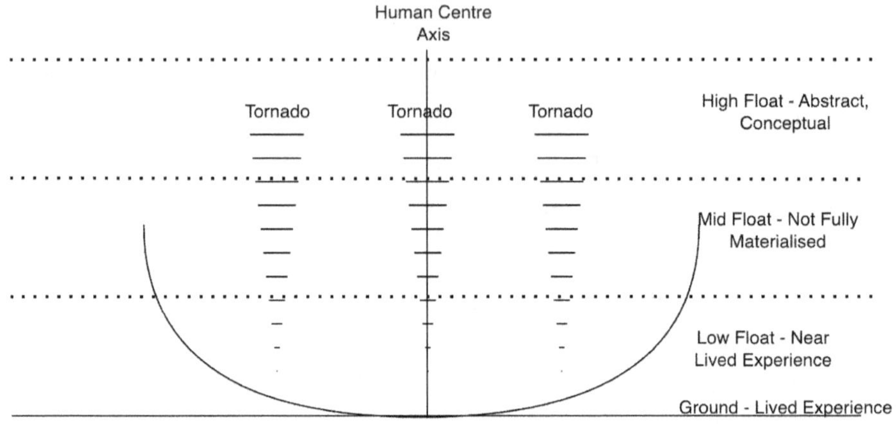

— —

Pattern Interpretation and Mapping

The concave bowl functions as a containment basin. Like a physical bowl, it gathers rather than generates. Skinwalker Ranch does not behave as an origin point, but as a receiver where disparate phenomena accumulate and express.

Because the bowl spans left, centre, and right, the phenomena engage relational, human, and abstract layers simultaneously. Its grounded nature ties it to land, geology, and long-standing environmental conditions. The ranch behaves as a natural convergence basin, pulling in unrelated effects and allowing them to manifest in proximity without a single underlying cause.

This alone explains why so many unrelated phenomena are reported at the same location.

— —

The three vertical tornadoes represent recurrent channels. Their helical form indicates dynamic transfer rather than static presence. These are not pillars; they are conduits. They suggest continuous coupling and decoupling between layers of reality.

The bowl holds the three tornadoes across left, centre, and right.
- The left column corresponds to animal anomalies, trickster narratives, shapeshifter stories, and subjective experiences that resist instrumentation.
- The centre column corresponds to human responses: fear, confusion, time distortion, and physiological effects. This explains why activity often escalates when observers are present and why experiences appear tied to attention.
- The right column corresponds to electromagnetic anomalies, sensor irregularities, equipment failures, and inconsistent measurement results.

— —

Skinwalker Ranch feels chaotic because the bowl collects while the tornadoes activate independently. This produces incoherence, contradiction, volatility, and narrative overload—precisely what is reported.

No single story can resolve the site. The left column generates relational anomalies, the centre destabilises witnesses, and the right teases measurement without closure. This is why the ranch produces vast amounts of data without resolution.

——

When individuals strongly identify with one channel—through fear, fixation, belief, or obsessive measurement—they may continue to perceive effects elsewhere. This is not because something follows them, but because they remain tuned to that channel. This maps cleanly to reports of phenomena "following" investigators.

——

Skinwalker Ranch is best understood as a naturally occurring convergence zone where environmental conditions allow intermittent, chaotic coupling between relational, human, and physical layers. The result is fragmentation rather than communication.

Earlier left-side cultures would not have investigated such a place. They would have marked it as unstable, restricted access, adjusted migration routes, or established avoidance taboos—not because it was evil, but because nothing coherent could be lived there.

Modern humans attempt to interrogate, narrativise, and weaponise it. The land does not respond well to that approach.

Bermuda Triangle

The Bermuda Triangle is a loosely defined region in the western North Atlantic Ocean, commonly described as spanning Miami

(Florida), Bermuda, and San Juan (Puerto Rico). A number of aircraft and ships have disappeared under unusual circumstances within this area.

Stories of strange behaviour in the region date back as far as Christopher Columbus. However, the incident that cemented the Bermuda Triangle's modern infamy was the disappearance of Flight 19 in 1945. A squadron of five U.S. Navy training bombers departed Fort Lauderdale on a routine navigation exercise. During the flight, the leader, Lieutenant Charles Taylor, reported that his compasses had failed and that he could no longer determine their position. All five aircraft vanished. A rescue plane sent to locate them also disappeared that same night. In total, 27 men and six aircraft were lost within a single evening.

Over the decades, additional disappearances and navigation incidents accumulated, giving rise to a wide range of explanations. Paranormal theories have included remnants of Atlantean technology interfering with electronics, anomalous Earth magnetic effects, time warps, portals, and alien abductions similar to the Betty and Barney Hill or Travis Walton narratives.

Scientific explanations range from there being no mystery at all, to combinations of powerful ocean currents, rogue waves, sudden storms, waterspouts, and methane gas releases capable of reducing water buoyancy and sinking vessels rapidly.

— —

Pattern Reading

Shape:

Tall, thin, solid oval

Straddling centre and off-centre left

This geometry immediately indicates that the phenomenon is neither an intelligence nor an intervention. It is a stable channel intersecting specific sensory bands.

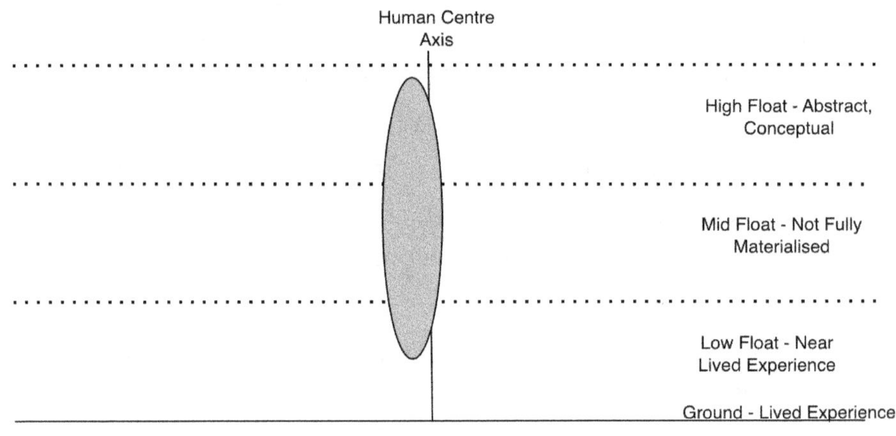

——

Pattern Interpretation and Mapping

The Bermuda Triangle is not an entity, not a place that "does something," and not a decision-making system.

A tall oval in a geographic context indicates duration across time rather than a discrete event. It represents continuity — a passage or corridor — not rupture. Its thinness indicates a narrow tolerance: most traffic passes nearby without incident. Its solidity suggests the condition is reliable and repeatable rather than random.

Placement straddling the left and centre axes is key. The left side indicates a relational, environmental field condition that does not present itself cleanly to abstraction or instrumentation. The centre intersection means that humans directly experience its effects.

This is not a phenomenon acting on the world. It is a boundary condition that human systems occasionally cross.

Functionally, the oval describes a zone of containment without edges. It is not a portal, not a trap, and not a location where things are taken. It is an area where orientation thins.

Within this zone:
- Navigation coherence degrades
- Instrument readings decouple from environmental reality
- Time, direction, and reference lose rigidity

Nothing attacks. Nothing chooses. Nothing decides. Systems simply fail to stay aligned.

— —

Disappearances are intermittent because the oval does not fill the region. It likely becomes active only when certain environmental conditions coincide with human systems that depend heavily on abstraction — instruments, charts, and assumed consistency.

Earlier navigators, who relied more on relational sensing and environmental cues, would pass through with fewer losses. This helps explain why Columbus could note unusual behaviour yet continue without catastrophe. Modern navigation systems expect stable reference. When that stability thins, failure becomes sudden and severe.

——

No single explanation fully resolves the phenomenon because each interpretive layer fails differently. Left-side field conditions leave no evidence. Centre-axis disruption appears as human error. Right-side instruments produce contradictory or misleading data. As a result, explanations fragment into weather, magnetism, methane gas, aliens, or portals — each capturing a partial effect while mistaking it for cause.

——

Returning to Flight 19: nothing "paranormal" likely occurred. What happened was predictable given the nature of the Bermuda Triangle.

They did not vanish.
They lost centre orientation.

For centre-anchored humans, a left–centre coherence corridor dissolves the internal sense of "this is where I am." The experience would have been confusion rather than drama — the horizon feeling wrong, headings not agreeing, landmarks refusing to resolve, and instruments contradicting one another.

With navigation systems decoupled from environmental reality, the loss of orientation compounded. Flight 19 drifted off course with no reliable means of recalibration. They continued flying until fuel was exhausted.

The wreckage was never found not because it disappeared, but because it ended up somewhere no one thought to look.

Out-Of-Place Artefacts

Voynich Manuscript

The Voynich Manuscript has baffled researchers for decades and is widely considered the world's most mysterious book. It is a handwritten and illustrated manuscript from the early 15th century, written in an unknown script and containing drawings of plants, celestial forms, and biological scenes that do not correspond to known systems. It originally contained 272 pages, of which 240 remain, many of them large fold-outs. Every serious attempt at translation has failed.

The manuscript is named after Wilfrid Voynich, a Polish-American book dealer who purchased it from a Jesuit college in Italy in 1912. Inside the book was a letter dated 1665, written by a scientist seeking help in deciphering the manuscript. The book is currently housed at the Beinecke Rare Book & Manuscript Library at Yale University.

Unlike many anomalous artefacts, the Voynich Manuscript is well-grounded materially. Carbon dating of the animal-skin pages places its creation around 1400 AD. The ink and pigments are consistent with materials available in Central Europe during the Renaissance. The mystery is not its physical origin, but its orientation.

The manuscript is heavily illustrated, and based on its imagery, researchers have divided it into apparent sections: herbal, astronomical, biological, cosmological, and pharmaceutical. These divisions make visual sense, even though the text remains unreadable.

Professional codebreakers, linguists, and cryptographers have all failed to decode it. Popular theories range from medieval medical shorthand, to a lost language, to a hoax, to non-human authorship. More recently, artificial intelligence has been applied to the text, also without success.

— —

Pattern Readings

Two pattern readings were applied to the Voynich Manuscript.

Pattern 1 — The Manuscript as an Artefact

Shapes
- Right side: Hill
- Left side: Floating quarter-circle

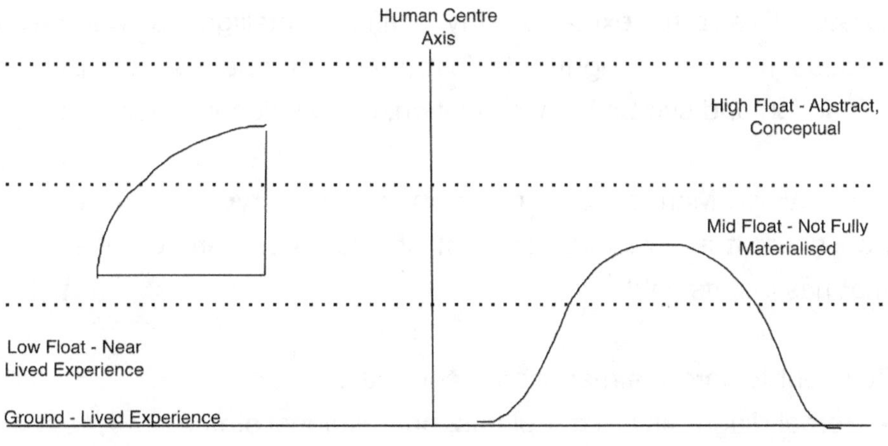

The right-side hill represents accumulated effort. This maps to decades of scholarly, linguistic, cryptographic, and technical labour applied to the manuscript. A hill indicates gradual accumulation without breakthrough. There is no singular hidden key waiting to be cracked. Each decoding attempt adds interpretive mass, but no attempt resolves the manuscript. The Voynich absorbs right-side effort without yielding to it.

The left-side floating quarter-circle explains why. The manuscript is predominantly a left-side artefact.

A quarter-circle represents partial containment. It holds coherence, but not in a closed or fully encoded way. Its left-side placement indicates relational or perceptual knowing rather than instructional or propositional knowledge. Floating indicates it is no longer grounded in land, ritual, or lived continuity. It has been severed from the perceptual field that once made it legible.

The manuscript was never meant to be decoded in isolation. It made sense only within a living relational context that no longer exists. This also explains why artificial intelligence will never decode it. AI is a right-side instrument. It operates on pattern extraction and symbolic manipulation, not relational coherence.

The Voynich Manuscript is not a hoax, not encrypted text, and not nonsense. It is a residual artefact of a left-side perceptual system that has lost its field.

To orient toward the manuscript correctly:
- Herbal diagrams are not plants, but relational states.
- The text is not language, but rhythmic anchoring.

• Symbols function as orientation cues, not representations.

Once the perceptual field collapsed, the manuscript became opaque. Its coherence cannot be reconstructed without the conditions that once held it.

——

Pattern 2 — The World Implied by the Manuscript

Shape
Right side: Small, floating, faded pyramid (low)

A pyramid represents hierarchy and structured knowledge. The world implied by the Voynich had order, domains, and layered understanding. It was not chaotic or mystical in the modern sense.

The pyramid is small, indicating limited scope. This was not a civilisation-wide system, but a bounded community or specialised group — a closed ecology of practice.

Faded indicates the structure is no longer active. This is not destruction or suppression. It is natural decay after function completed. Floating shows the system is no longer grounded in land, practice, or daily life. Low placement indicates proximity to embodiment and practicality, which maps to the manuscript's focus on plants, bodies, cycles, and cosmology.

This explains why the world implied by the Voynich feels coherent yet unreachable. It was once functional, but its grounding conditions disappeared.

Taken together, the two patterns indicate the manuscript is complete — not unfinished, not broken — but divorced from the field that allowed it to operate. It is a finished artefact whose mode of use no longer exists.

Antikythera Mechanism

The Antikythera Mechanism was a portable, wooden-cased device about the size of a shoebox. It featured complex bronze displays on both its front and back faces. The front was circular and planetarium-like, with multiple pointers showing the positions of the Sun, Moon, and five known planets. The back featured two large spiral dials that tracked lunar and eclipse cycles. On the side was a hand crank that, when turned, activated multiple interlocking internal gears, moving all the astronomical displays in precise synchronisation.

The mechanism was discovered in a shipwreck in 1901. Divers exploring a Roman wreck off the coast of the Greek island of Antikythera recovered it among statues and pottery. For decades it sat largely ignored in a museum, because historians believed ancient Greeks lacked the technology to manufacture complex gear systems. It was not until the 1970s, when researchers applied X-ray imaging and later 3D reconstruction, that its true nature became clear.

The device dates to roughly 150–100 BC. No specific maker has been identified.

The mystery is not the device itself, but the absence of its predecessors. The mechanism is so sophisticated that it could not have been a one-off creation. Engineering of this precision requires a long period of experimentation and refinement. Yet we have found no simpler machines leading up to it. It is as if we discovered a smartphone buried among the Terracotta Warriors of China.

— —

Pattern Reading

Shape:
- Left-side solid wedge
- ~5-degree tilt
- One side touching the centre axis
- Point touching centre bottom (ground)

— —

Pattern Interpretation and Mapping

A left-side solid wedge places the mechanism firmly in a relational, distributed orientation. It was not built to convey symbolic meaning, nor to store abstract knowledge. It was built to mediate relationships — between cycles, time, sky, land, and human action.

A wedge is not a container and not a narrative. It is an interface tool. Something inserted to allow two systems to meet at the correct angle.

This tells us the Antikythera Mechanism was not:
- a curiosity item
- a one-off invention
- an early "computer" in the modern sense

It was a calibration device.

The slight five-degree tilt indicates deliberate asymmetry. The world it was built for was understood as almost regular, but never perfectly aligned. This maps cleanly to lunar irregularities, eclipse cycles, planetary retrograde motion, and seasonal drift. The device does not enforce perfection; it compensates for deviation.

One side touching the centre axis means the mechanism directly interfaces with human use. It was meant to be handled, consulted, and referenced in lived time. It was likely used in navigation, agriculture, civic planning, and the timing of rituals.

The point touching the centre bottom anchors the entire system in embodied time. Not cosmic time. Not divine time. Human time lived on Earth. The mechanism did not predict the heavens for their own sake — it told humans when to act in relation to celestial cycles.

The Antikythera Mechanism was a left-side calibration wedge that allowed humans to remain aligned with complex astronomical rhythms. It sat between sky, land, cycles, decision-making, perception, and action. It was not mythic, and it was not purely scientific in the modern sense.

A civilisation capable of building this had an intact distributed perceptual orientation alongside sufficient right-side mechanical skill. This also explains why the mechanism did not reproduce as a continuing tradition. Once distributed orientation faded, the wedge had nowhere to insert itself.

The device became unintelligible not because it was too advanced, but because the perceptual environment it was designed to serve disappeared.

Iron Pillar of Delhi

The Iron Pillar of Delhi is a 24-foot-tall structure in the Qutb Complex, India. Made of 98% wrought iron and weighing over six tonnes, it is more than 1,600 years old and has resisted rusting despite centuries of exposure to monsoon rains and humidity.

Constructed during the Gupta Empire, its Sanskrit inscription states it was erected as a "Standard of Vishnu" to honour a king named Chandra. Early speculation suggested a "lost metal," but metallurgical analysis in the 2000s revealed that its phosphorus content formed a thin, protective layer called misawite. This layer reforms if scratched, effectively preserving the iron.

The question remains: Was it a monument? Or something else entirely?

——

Pattern Reading

Far left — tall vertical pillar. Grounded.

This is not just persistence. It is active coherence holding.

——

Pattern Interpretation and Mapping

Placed far left, the pillar exists apart from narrative. It does not communicate, teach, or represent. It functions whether anyone notices.

Vertical indicates phase alignment across layers. Its role was maintaining stability over long time scales — slow oscillations that show across generations.

Tall shows the stabilisation endured centuries. Grounded ties it to land and ecology, embedding its effect in environment and human presence without management. It stabilised relational field coherence — land, climate, and human systems — preventing gradual drift.

Today, it appears "just a pillar." The distributed orientation system that gave it purpose has decayed, leaving a residual effect. Its rust resistance is not the function itself, but a visible marker of its ongoing presence.

This mirrors the Antikythera mechanism: both make sense only within an intact distributed orientation.

The Baghdad Battery

The Baghdad Battery is a set of artefacts discovered near Baghdad in the 1930s:

- A clay jar - A small, 5-inch-tall oval-shaped pot made of bright yellow clay.

- A copper cylinder - A tube made of a thin copper sheet that was placed inside the jar.
- An iron rod - A small iron rod suspended inside the copper cylinder, held in place by an asphalt plug that sealed the top of the jar.

Found in Iraq that some researchers believe represents a form of ancient electrical technology dating back over 2,000 years. If true, it would predate the invention of the modern battery by nearly 1,600 years.

The theory is that the jar functioned as a galvanic cell if filled with an acidic liquid (like lemon juice, vinegar). A chemical reaction would occur between the copper and the iron. This would result in electricity generation. Modern scientists have built replicas using these exact materials and successfully produced a measurable electric current.

Mainstream archaeology remains very cautious about calling this a "battery". Similar storage jarsfound in the region were used to store scrolls. The components might simply be a protective casing for an ancient document that has since rotted away. There are no ancient writings or drawings describing electricity or its use.

— —

Pattern Reading

Left side: Small faded triangle. Grounded.

— —

Pattern Interpretation and Mapping

The left-side placement indicates this is not a technological breakthrough narrative. It is relational and contextual, not progressive. The shape does not point toward technological advancement, rather it points sideways toward forgotten relational continuity.

The triangle suggests a functional minimum. Three elements. No excess. Just enough structure to do something.

Its faded quality matters means this is not an active system. It is not calling attention to itself. It is residue.

The Baghdad Battery does not imply a lost civilisation of advanced engineers. It indicates something more mundane - localised, practical knowledge that did not propagate, scale, or self-identify as technology as we understand it.

The strongest theory supporting its use, given the low resulting voltage, is electroplating. Small scale gold electroplating can be achieved with very low voltage, exactly in the range these jars produce. If correct, the battery was not used for power, lighting, or machines. But for finishing artisan objects — ornamentation, ritual items, or status goods. This places the battery in the left-side domain with ritual and relational function. Not abstraction. Not theory. Not infrastructure.

The discomfort modern science feels around the Baghdad Battery comes from category violation. Electricity is treated as a late abstraction, something that must arrive alongside scientific method. The battery violates that assumption by suggesting function without theory. The person(s) using it may have known that it works without knowing why it works. That is simply non-right-sided.

The faded triangle also suggests fragility. This knowledge did not self-preserve. It did not become tradition.   It likely existed in pockets, transmitted through apprenticeship or ritual practice, and eventually disappeared. This is why the Baghdad Battery feels like an anomaly rather than evidence. It left no lineage.

The Baghdad Battery does not ask us to rewrite history. It asks us to soften its boundaries. Human knowledge has not moved in a clean upward line from "primitive" to sophistication. The Baghdad Battery is not proof of ancient advanced civilisation. It is proof that our definition of "advanced" is narrower than it needs to be.

A Final Orientation

Perception is an ongoing relationship between a human nervous system, a culture, and the world we find ourselves in. What this book has pointed to is not a hidden layer of reality, but a forgotten way of relating to what is already here — a way of noticing that once preceded explanation, and was later replaced by interpretation. Perception reorganised itself for survival. And it continues to reorganise itself through every era, technological shift, and worldview we inhabit.

Human perception has constraints. We resolve ambiguity through a narrow funnel shaped by biology, survival, and culture. When uncertainty enters, it collapses into familiar forms. These forms persist because they stabilise experience enough to be shared, remembered, and acted upon. Repetition is not evidence of the sameness of anomalies, but evidence of perceptual convergence.

Resolution keeps failing not because the mysteries are unsolvable, but because the mode being used to resolve them is mismatched to the phenomena themselves. Right-side tools seek containment, explanation, and closure. Many of the phenomena explored in this book do not exist to be narrativised. They arise at boundaries — between perception and interpretation, between environment and observer, and between coherence and its loss. When resolution is forced, meaning collapses into narrative, belief, fear, or authority. What remains unresolved is not the phenomenon, but our discomfort with leaving perception open.

This is where agency returns to you. You do not need to adopt a belief, accept a theory, or replace one explanation with another.

The invitation here is quieter.
It is to notice how you notice.

To see where you reach for narrative, where you default to established stories, and where you allow ambiguity to remain intact. The mysteries are not what we thought they were — flying saucers, mythic beings and creatures, mysterious places and objects. They are in how we relate to what we encounter. And in doing so, the real mystery surfaces: the nature of the reality we live in.

This book traced a path. It showed that a different way of perceiving once existed. That it was outgrown. And that its absence left afterimages wherever humans brush against the edges of reality without the perceptual structures to hold it. In following that path, the aim was not to restore what was lost, but to make its absence felt and visible.

You do not need to agree with everything in these pages. That was never the point. If something here reorganised how you noticed — even slightly — then the work has already done what it needed to do.

Appendix: On Perceptual Method

The structural shapes used in this book were not learned as a technique, nor accessed through belief or visualisation. They emerged as a byproduct of sustained work with narrative itself.

Extended Jungian shadow work trained an ability to remain present with conflicting interpretations, emotional charge, and unresolved meaning without prematurely collapsing them into story. Over time, this created a stable internal environment where narratives could be held without being inhabited.

Once narrative pressure reduced, underlying structures began to register on their own. Not as images or messages, but as constraints. Simple relational configurations that limited what could reasonably arise.

The shapes described throughout this book are not symbolic, and they are not personal. They function as orientation markers that appear when interpretation is suspended long enough for structure to become evident.

This way of perceiving is not presented as special. It is a consequence of learning how not to interfere or identify with meaning while it is forming.

Readers are not asked to adopt this method. The book can be read without it. The consistency of the mappings stands or falls on its own.

— —-

The author currently lives in Melbourne, Australia, and may be contacted on:
fieldcartographer@proton.me